"Mastering Adulthood does a masterful job of bringing timeless wisdom and practical solutions to young adults. Current social and economic conditions can seem challenging to young people who seek to live lives of meaning, purpose, and joy. Fielding provides evidence-based methods, humor, and practical enlightenment for those facing these hurdles. In fact, this user-friendly guidebook for living with mindful purpose could help just about anybody, at any stage of life."

> —**Dennis Tirch, PhD**, author of *The Compassionate-Mind Guide to Overcoming Anxiety*, and founder of The Center for Compassion Focused Therapy

"Finally, a 'how-to' book for transition age adults. So often manuals with behavioral skills are either too young or too old for eighteen- to twenty-five-year-olds. Fielding uses examples, stories, and practices that will resonate with people who are entering adulthood. *Mastering Adulthood* combines mindfulness and current emotion regulation strategies in a practical, easy-to-use format. This book can be used by young adults alone, with others, or in a counseling setting. I have begun to use the dashboard practices and the pauses with my own clients."

> —**Shari Manning, PhD**, CEO and founder of Treatment Implementation Collaborative and SC Center for Dialectical Behavior Therapy, and author of *Loving Someone with Borderline Personality Disorder*

"Adulthood is becoming more complicated. All of us need help, and Lara E. Fielding has written a wonderful guide. *Mastering Adulthood* will teach readers how patterned habits keep us stuck, how to then develop new and more effective behaviors, and the practice of mindfulness as the key to establishing a more grounded and emotionally attuned life."

> —**Blaise Aguirre, MD**, medical director of 3East DBT-Continuum at McLean Hospital, assistant professor in the department of psychiatry at Harvard Medical School, and coauthor of *Mindfulness for Borderline Personality Disorder* and *Coping with BPD*

"I could not love this book more! Fielding beautifully weaves case examples, personal experience, research, and brilliant use of metaphor into a fun, easy-to-digest book designed to help young adults tackle the psychological complexities of growing into emotionally competent, independent adults. While the language and examples are geared toward a twentysomething to thirtysomething audience, any individual interested in greater self-knowledge and psychological growth can benefit from the evidence-based concepts in *Mastering Adulthood*—I know I did!"

—**Jill A. Stoddard, PhD**, director of The Center for Stress and Anxiety Management in San Diego, CA, and coauthor of *The Big Book of ACT Metaphors*

"Lara Fielding's enthusiasm for helping those who wish to have an engaging and meaningful adult life shines through in *Mastering Adulthood*. Her ability to guide you through learning how to develop and practice psychological flexibility, as well as emotion management, is skillful. She has created a book grounded in solid evidence of psychological theory and practice that will help those grappling with "adulting" find new ways to cope with the realities of adulthood in a fast-paced world. For those thousands of people seeking guidance on how to successfully navigate this thing called living, Fielding expertly teaches you how to get in the driver's seat and steer toward success!"

—**Robyn D. Walser, PhD**, licensed clinical psychologist; coauthor of *Learning ACT*, *The Mindful Couple*, *Acceptance and Commitment Therapy for the Treatment of Post-Traumatic Stress Disorder and Trauma-Related Problems*; and author of *The Heart of ACT*

"There is more to adulthood than handling its instrumental challenges. If you stop there, you will never learn how to create the kind of life you really want. This comprehensive and cleverly organized book invites you to look more deeply at your habits of handling emotions, to find what really motivates you, and then to construct the skills you need build your life around deeper goals: relationships that matter, work that prospers, a profound connection with life. Adulthood doesn't come with an owner's manual—you need to explore what makes you tick and draft your own. This book will help. Highly recommended."

—**Steven C. Hayes, PhD**, professor in the department of psychology at the University of Nevada, developer of acceptance and commitment therapy, and author of *Get Out of Your Mind and Into Your Life*

"This is the book I needed to grow up. Here is help to know what truly matters, what you truly care about. And with clarity about core values comes motivation and a surer sense of direction. Of equal importance is how *Mastering Adulthood* helps you overcome the emotional and mental roadblocks—those nasty passengers everyone carries—that sometimes keep you from fully embracing life. This masterful book, based on the principles of acceptance and commitment therapy (ACT), can throw open the doors to becoming a vital, self-directed grown-up."

—**Matthew McKay, PhD**, coauthor of *Mind and Emotions*

MASTERING ADULTHOOD

GO BEYOND ADULTING
TO BECOME AN
EMOTIONAL GROWN-UP

LARA FIELDING, PsyD

NEW HARBINGER PUBLICATIONS, INC.

Publisher's Note

Rumi, excerpt from "The Guesthouse," translated by Coleman Barks. Copyright © 1997 by Coleman Barks. Used by permission.

Distributed in Canada by Raincoast Books

Copyright © 2019 by Lara E. Fielding
New Harbinger Publications, Inc.
5674 Shattuck Avenue
Oakland, CA 94609
www.newharbinger.com

Cover design by Amy Shoup

Acquired by Elizabeth Hollis Hansen

Edited by Gretel Hakanson

MIX
Paper from
responsible sources
FSC
www.fsc.org
FSC® C011935

Library of Congress Cataloging-in-Publication Data

Names: Fielding, Lara E., author.
Title: Mastering adulthood : go beyond adulting to become an emotional grown-up / Lara E. Fielding.
Description: Oakland, CA : New Harbinger Publications, 2019. | Includes bibliographical references.
Identifiers: LCCN 2018031429 (print) | LCCN 2018032654 (ebook) | ISBN 9781684031948 (PDF e-book) | ISBN 9781684031955 (ePub) | ISBN 9781684031931 (paperback)
Subjects: LCSH: Adulthood--Psychological aspects. | Emotions. | Stress management. | Self-actualization (Psychology) | BISAC: PSYCHOLOGY / Developmental / Adulthood & Aging. | SELF-HELP / Personal Growth / Happiness. | SELF-HELP / Stress Management.
Classification: LCC BF724.5 (ebook) | LCC BF724.5 .F54 2019 (print) | DDC 155.67--dc23
LC record available at https://lccn.loc.gov/2018031429

21   20   19

10   9   8   7   6   5   4   3   2   1   First Printing

To my Ruben –

For providing so much support and evidence to the contrary…

My passengers could no longer get in the way

of this lifelong valued outcome.

Thank You!

And

In loving memory of

the one who guided me,

and was instrumental to the adult I became:

R. Scott Brooks.

Never Forgotten.

Contents

PART IV: Successful You: Maintaining Commitment to Yourself and Others

Introduction

Good job! You picked up this book!

Maybe you're a seeker. Maybe you know you have a life purpose. Perhaps you even have an inkling of what it is, but you're having a hard time getting traction to go in the right direction. Something keeps getting in the way of you mastering this thing called adulthood. You might be having a hard time with motivation, or anxiety and mood, which keeps you from getting where you want to go in life, and that only makes you less motivated or more anxious and moody, right?

When you've got the pressure of building your whole life ahead of you, unmotivated and moody is a rotten place to be! Mastering adulthood has always been tough, but never like it is today. In this digital age, everything's moving faster, the stakes are higher, and the competition is steeper. Making things worse, in an attention-deprived world, there's often less available meaningful support than you might feel you need.

This combination of stress factors is leaving a lot of people feeling really off their game and desperate for tools to cope with the new realities of adulthood. Does this sound like you? Are difficult emotions, like anxiety, sadness, and anger, or even just a lack of motivation and uncertainty, getting in the way of your goals and life purpose? If so, you're in the right place!

If you picked up this book, I'm guessing you want more from your existence than just adulting—more than slogging through the mundane responsibilities of being a grown-up just waiting for the fun part. Sure, knowing how to take care of your adult self is important. But more important, why might the things you've got to do be important to *you*?

This book is all about taking a deeper look under the hood of your life, figuring out what makes you tick, and building the skills you need to respond most effectively, rather than just habitually, when you have to "adult." This book will help you actively construct the life *you* want so you're not just existing your way along, dodging and weaving around what life throws at you!

Beyond Labels: Getting at the Root

You may or may not have an anxiety or mood disorder. This book isn't about any particular diagnosis. The info here applies to everyone, whether you have an actual diagnosis, just want to promote your mental health resilience, or prevent a relapse. Diagnostic labels are like flowers in a pot. They're just what we see on the surface. But at the bottom of that pot, there's a system that regulates how the flowers emerge. *That's* what we're working with in this book!

Because we're all in this thing called "being human" together, we all experience some degree of anxiety or mood symptoms during the course of our life. So, the underlying science of how we get stuck and the tools we need to get unstuck can help *anybody*. These skills are not just a Band-Aid for symptoms; they're about getting at the *root cause* within the mind-body system, which can cause anyone's emotion system to get out of whack.

The scientific term for what we're tackling here is *emotion dysregulation*, which is the root cause of the motivation, moods, and anxiety you experience. It doesn't mean you're a crazed maniac who can't control yourself. (Although it could look like that.) Your emotion regulation system is more nuanced than that. *Emotion regulation* is the ability to flexibly adjust to the demands of the environment (Gross and Munoz 1995). When there are big life changes, causing you stress (like going off to or finishing school, starting a job, leaving a relationship, or making any major life decisions), the emotion regulation system naturally gets strained. So you need more flexibility in order to adapt to the changes than when life is consistent.

Stress and change (or the need for change) make it more likely for the system to get out of sync, which can affect your ability to regulate your emotions. You know that feeling when you are really anxious, sad, or pissed off about something, and you just can't shake it? Or when you know there is something you want to get moving on but can't seem to? Or when it just feels like life is an endless cycle of the same old, same old? Those are signs that your regulator is stuck.

But here's the less intuitive part: someone whose emotion system is dysregulated could be either an underregulator or an overregulator! When you're underregulated, you notice it more; it shows up in classic signs of mood and anxiety: sadness, irritability, and maybe even panic attacks. Overregulation, on the other hand, comes with a whole slew of other problems. When you're overregulated, you might not really feel sad or anxious per se, but you're more likely to feel "blah," unmotivated, or just not excited about what life has to offer. Because of the habitual ways in which we respond to stress, the root problem is that *the regulator gets rigid*.

Getting Unstuck with Mindfulness

Unsticking the regulator is where mindfulness skills come in. You may have heard some of the chatter about this newly trendy and ancient practice of holding attention, in the present moment, nonjudgmentally. There's a ton of science showing that mindfulness skills can help you develop the kind of nonreactive but engaged attention you need to hold it together in the face of the stress of setting up your life. It's become very popular with everyone from athletes to executives and celebrities to CEOs. And yes, mindfulness practices improve mood and anxiety disorders too.

With multiple screens in our face the majority of our waking hours, our attention muscles are withering. With the world literally in the palm of your hand, how do you decide where to allocate your attention first? How can you stay committed to the things you want and not get overwhelmed by all the distractions in this new era of adulthood? And

I do mean, *How?* The pragmatic mindfulness and self-care skills you'll learn here will put you in the driver's seat of your attention and emotions and teach you *how* to prevent them from getting the best of you. These practices will give you the *felt sense* of what being skillful is like.

Keeping It Experiential

The skills in this book come from the most evidence-supported mindfulness-based cognitive behavioral therapies (CBTs) for stress and problems with emotion regulation (sometimes referred to as the *third wave* of CBT). One of the *most important* elements for lasting change is to make the exercises as *experiential* as possible for you. So, I've taken the practices up and off the page to bring them to life! Throughout the book, you'll find QR codes, such as the one below. Simply aim your smartphone camera at the QR code to automatically link to related video clips (http://mindful-mastery.com/book/videos). If you ever have a question about a particular skill practice, just shoot me a message in the comments section beneath the video! You'll also find the worksheets and guided imagery audio exercises you'll need here at http://www.newharbinger.com/41931.

Why I'm Excited to Help: A Bit About Me

As you can see, I get really excited about sharing the skills I teach in my private practice and to graduate students as an adjunct professor at Pepperdine University. The reason I'm so excited about sharing them is because I have seen firsthand how commitment to learning and practicing them can change lives.

I've also seen how not having these skills has destroyed lives. My own early adult years, although another era, were filled with extreme competition, social comparisons, and lack of support. I became a psychologist because I saw people I loved succumb to the strong emotions and the stressors of transitioning into adulthood. And I wasn't able to help them correct course. Helping those I can makes me really happy!

Quite honestly, I was terrified that I would lose my mental footing too. But I had a sneaking suspicion that our mental health had something to do with how we take care of ourselves. I believed intuitively, what the research now bears out, that the status of our mental health is strongly influenced by our day-to-day habits and how we cope with stress.

As perhaps you are experiencing, it took me a while to find my path. I dropped out of high school at fifteen, and it wasn't until I was past thirty that I started my studies at Santa Monica College. It was there that I began studying the psychobiology of stress and emotions. I knew I was onto something about how self-care influences mental health. I continued my studies of the psychophysiology of stress and emotions at UCLA and Harvard before getting my doctorate, specializing in mindfulness interventions, at Pepperdine.

Now, my life's work is about making the best practices in psychology accessible, affordable, and engaging to meet the needs of young adults. Whether you live in Compton or Beverly Hills, have an actual diagnosis, or just want to promote your mental health or prevent relapse, practicing these skills can get you there! These are the same skills I teach and coach my clients on to build emotion regulation and stress resilience. As I do in my office, I am here to suggest, encourage, cheerlead, and validate. But only you can take the steps needed to move forward on your unique path.

The Journey to Mastering Adulthood

The organization of this book will give you a clear road map of how to begin building balance into your regulation system and find what makes you happy. So whatever adulting challenges you're facing, the teachings and practices here can help you hurdle them. Each chapter will build upon the last, taking you a bit deeper into the information and practices of *how* to master your journey into, and beyond, adulting.

Part I: Waking Up to the Universal You

In part I of the book, we'll be mapping out the big-picture territory: why humans can naturally and very commonly get caught in psychological and emotional habits that keep us low in mood and motivation. Couched in a simple-to-understand metaphor, you'll learn how our holistic systems operate. Very important, you'll learn why our past influences our present but doesn't need to dictate it. It can be quite a relief to learn that we are all wired in a way that sets us up for some of our less glorious moments. So you can stop being so tough on yourself!

I'll share some examples of common ways our hardwiring can hijack us, which you may recognize in yourself. Ultimately, my hope is that by the end of the first section, you'll see that you are not "broken" or "crazy." (You may be unskillful, but we'll remedy that in part III.) We're all working with the same component parts. Understanding how your story gets caught in the system empowers you to begin making the changes you want.

Part II: Unique You

Part II is all about you! Here, we'll be diving in to uncover your blind spots and demystify how you tend to get stuck. The mindfulness practices will help you see how your unique life experiences have gotten programmed into the universal system. When you get to this section, you're going to want to do these practices because what's more fun than demystifying your own psyche? (Okay, maybe that is just my psychology geek coming out.) But seriously, just as we turn to experts for help with something they have studied and know a lot about, *you are the expert in you!* So, you'll get the most from this process if you take an active role in these practices.

Have you ever wondered, *Why does this keep happening to me?* Or maybe you just assume the mood and motivation rut you're in is "just how it is," or worse, "just how *you* are." Well, in this section, you'll get started in stepping out of that unhelpful belief. Here, you'll be doing the brave work of stepping back and gaining some clarity on the situations in your life. This self-awareness section will teach you to hack into your unique patterns and figure out where the barriers are coming from. I'll guide you to get clearer about your life direction so that you can make sure any hassles you come across are really worth it! You'll finish this section by identifying and setting up the commitments you need to get you moving in the right direction.

Part III: Skillful You

Part III is where the rubber hits the road: the skills you need to work more effectively with your emotions and motivation. If you make it to part III of the book, then you'll already be showing the bravery and commitment it takes to own your destiny! These skills dovetail directly into the universal system to help you override the automatic reaction patterns that get and keep you stuck.

Here, you'll find a treasure trove of skills to help you build a healthy, adaptive emotion system. Like a kid in the candy store, you can customize your own journey to mastering adulthood. Some of the skills are going to help you get through a tough moment without making it worse. Others are gentle ways of planting the seeds of resilience with self-validation and compassion. Still others are like squats for your mood and motivation—they aren't like a party when you're doing them, but they are an investment in your resilience and long-term mental wellness.

This isn't your mom's kind of self-help book, where you'll feel great just as long as you're reading it. You will *not* be getting any of that "Connecting to your higher conscious spirit of lightness, breathe into your deepest being of true inner wisdom, and be one with the Universe" kind of stuff, which makes me crazy. It may *feel* really great while you're reading it, but it does *nothing* to guide you in building objective self-awareness and learning *how* to be skillful toward your life goals: the great relationship, the awesome career, and the connected life experiences. The skills here are actually based on science and will help you build resilience and thrive on the long road of adulthood!

Part IV: Successful You

Just like any other healthy lifestyle choices, maintaining psychological flexibility and a healthy emotion regulation system takes support and commitment. Today more than ever, in our super-connected global village, every success story has a support team behind it. Our relationships are a huge part of our emotional well-being and reaching our goals. In this section, you'll learn how to apply your skills with others in order to build relationships that last while also meeting your needs.

In the last chapter, all the pieces will come together! By this point, it will be clear: human beings naturally revert to old familiar rigid habitual modes. So we're going to set you up for success with a personalized plan for maintaining mindful-mastery in your life. Here you'll be matching up your unique triggers and habit patterns (which you will identify in part II) with the emotional self-care skills (from part III) to maintain a healthy, flexible regulation system so you can stay committed to the adult life you truly want!

Are You Ready to Solve the Great Mystery of You?

Just as I do in my office, this book will ask you to sift through your experiences. While I cannot listen to your story directly, I will ask you questions so you may hear the answers for yourself, and in this way, you will tend to yourself as I would.

This process of asking questions and hearing your own responses will be in the form of "Pause" practices and questions that you will answer in a journal you keep with this book. I strongly encourage you to complete these exercises as best you can. Not completing the questions (even if you think you are answering them in your head) would be tantamount to your therapist or mentor not listening to you and not hearing your needs. It might be a nice symbolic act to buy a special journal to honor this journey you're beginning. The intention of any self-help book is for it to be used as a guide to help you be there for yourself, and for you to honor that responsibility. The question now is, Are you ready and willing to begin this adventure of self-exploration and solving the great mystery of you?

PAUSE. What do you notice? Do you have any particular reaction to this call to action? Do you feel energized, hesitant, skeptical? Whether you're feeling excited, skeptical, curious, or daunted, can you begin the first essential step in any journey? Can you practice willingness to move forward?

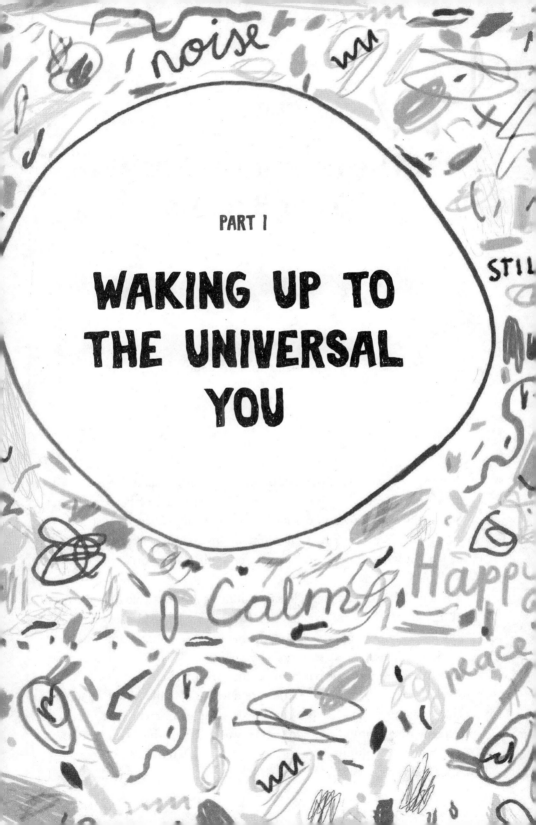

PART I

WAKING UP TO THE UNIVERSAL YOU

CHAPTER 1

The Emotional Habits That Bind Us

We are what we repeatedly do. Excellence, then, is not an act, but a habit.

—Aristotle

It was 11:47 p.m. when my phone showed Jessica's name for the third time that Tuesday night. Phone coaching was part of her treatment plan, so it wasn't so unusual for her to be calling. Even though it was late in the evening, I had intentionally invited my therapy clients to reach out when they're struggling to be skillful and worry that lack of skill may make a situation worse.

The concern I had with Jessica calling again was twofold. It was her third call. We had run through skills to practice twice already that day. But more important, the unhelpful habit we were targeting was the copious amounts of reassurance she tended to seek, which frequently led to her burning out her relationships with friends and loved ones. Jessica's deepest wish and goal of therapy was to build better relationships and overcome her profound fears of abandonment. We were in agreement that in order to do that, it was essential that she learn how to work more skillfully from the inside, rather than overrely on reassurance from the outside.

In that moment, looking down at my phone, I had to choose: answer the phone and reduce Jessica's despair, simultaneously relieving my own empathic distress, but certainly reinforcing her reassurance-seeking behavior, or not answer and risk triggering her most difficult feelings of abandonment. I was confident that on our previous calls we had reviewed three skills to practice, which she had used before successfully. I didn't answer the phone. I had to allow her the opportunity to practice her skills and learn that she could handle her emotions without resorting to her old emotional habit. The next day when I saw her in session, she reported being frustrated at first. And with a smirk of self-satisfaction she added, "Yeah, I know, I was skillful." After a quick high five, we moved on to the next topic.

Every day, each of us is tasked with the business of adulting—taking on the responsibilities that are the price of entry into the life we want to build while we're on the planet. Along the way, we're *all* faced with multiple decision points like the one Jessica and I faced that night. Just beneath the level of awareness, we are bid to respond to, react to, and engage with the world in a particular way. Should I follow the impulse to listen to an emotional need? Or is it more effective toward my long-term goals and the life I want to build to choose to do something different? Sometimes we need to listen to, indulge, and flow with our emotional experience. Sometimes the most effective thing to do is to choose an alternative response. It is in the balance of these two alternatives that our life path can become defined by the emotional habits that bind us.

We Are Creatures of Habit

Like many of my clients, Jessica was having a tough time hurdling one of the many transitions facing her in setting up her life as an adult. In her case, moving away to college was the prompting event, which unmasked the emotional habit that was undermining her progress. There was nothing wrong with what she was doing. After all, it's not a bad thing to reach out for help when we're in distress. It's a pretty effective thing to do actually. Jessica was just doing what her parents had always encouraged her to do growing up. What good parent wouldn't encourage a child to reach out for help? The problem developed for Jessica, as it does for all of us, when something that used to work to get through her difficult feelings stopped working because the *context* of the situation had changed.

What Jessica couldn't see, as most of us can't, is that she had simply gotten caught in the basic automatic human processes that underlie our emotions and motivation. We are all prone to these traps because humans are hardwired for habit formation. For the most part, habits evolved to make our life easier. We don't need to actively think about the ordinary tasks we do every day. You get in your car and just drive. You brush your teeth while thinking about other things. You put your pants on without deliberate conscious awareness because it is a more efficient use of internal resources to do so! The more our brain can shift from conscious, intentional activities to habitual, automated ones, the more space is available for creative problem solving and new tasks. Habits are an excellent solution to our need for efficiency!

Habits get programmed by the natural and automatic human pull to do more of what feels good and avoid what feels bad. Simple enough. But this simplicity means that just about any way of thinking or doing can become a habit if it reduces discomfort or increases pleasure in some way and is repeated over time. Once a habit is entrenched, it becomes like a well-worn path of reactivity, pulling us toward automaticity. Associations are made, and an action or thought becomes an impulse-driven stimulus response.

To make things even more hairy, as our ways of doing, thinking, and feeling become more habitual and automatic, they also move outside of awareness. It seems like stuff "just happens." Jessica wasn't scheming with a conscious intention when she called or texted repeatedly. She was simply repurposing an old, worn-out habit of reassurance seeking.

The more automatic a habit pattern becomes, the more difficult it is to actually see it as just that: a habit pattern. We rarely see how what once worked to get our needs met is no longer working. We're caught in the cycle. All we recognize, before we start taking a deeper look, is that we're not happy, not progressing toward our goals, or just stuck and unmotivated. Sound familiar?

PAUSE. Take a moment to consider why you picked up this book. In what areas of your life do you feel stuck, unmotivated, or just not happy right now? Jot down a few lines in your journal.

The Solution Becomes the Problem

Eddie was referred to me to treat his major depression. He was struggling with all the classic symptoms of low mood: lack of interest, fatigue, and negative thinking, and sometimes he just didn't feel like living anymore. He was so uncomfortable that his days were spent eagerly trying to find ways to feel more good and less bad: sleeping, eating junk food, looking at Internet porn, or just spacing out watching TV. He was very lonely, but social situations made him anxious. So he avoided people he didn't know very well. In short, Eddie's life was consumed by his emotional habits. His solution to internal discomfort had become the problem.

Emotional habits are ways of thinking and doing that sacrifice long-term goals for immediate gratification. They may offer short-term relief from the pains of life. But they come at a long-term cost. Of course, some emotional habits are more obvious. Substance use and abuse, smoking, unhealthy eating, or out-of-control sexual practices might be the clearest examples. But just about any pattern of thinking and doing that reduces discomfort or increases pleasure can become problematic—if it starts to get in the way of things we care about.

WTF? What's the Function?

Emotional habits aren't "good habits" or "bad habits" in one lump judgment. Instead, the habits we're concerned about here are the ones that are so aimed at increasing comfort and reducing discomfort that they derail your authentic purpose and the adult life you want. Some of the more subtle emotional habits can sneak up on you as normal stuff all humans do. Who hasn't found themselves binge-streaming TV, getting lost in social media, or overindulging occasionally in food or drink? It's not *what* you do that's really the problem, but the purpose or *function* of the habit that starts to sabotage you.

Even seemingly "good" habits can become emotionally driven doing and thinking patterns that interfere with building the kind of inspired, vibrant, and fulfilling life we want. Perfectionism, overexercising, and workaholism are good examples. We all like to feel on our game, be at our best, and enjoy the praise that comes with our successes. But problems can also arise when we become overly dependent on these self-esteem boosters. Unwillingness to experience the vulnerability of uncertainty and disappointment can send us chasing the high, rather than following our authentic intentions.

PAUSE. Do you already have an idea of some of your own habits that may make you feel better in the short term but are not so helpful in moving you toward your long-term goals? Note these in your journal.

Scanning her Instagram feed, Nina's posts showed her rockin' her cool entertainment industry job, at dinner with her fab boyfriend, and smiling ear to ear. She definitely *seemed* to have it all together. But Nina's old emotional control habits were showing a little wear and tear as the anxiety and irritability were beginning to leak out. Nina came to see me at the insistence of her boyfriend, who worried about her growing tension.

She sauntered into my office cool and reserved. As a therapist, it's my job to read emotional cues and sense the needs of others. But I was having a hard time getting a read on Nina. Over the course of our work together, we discovered this was part of Nina's emotional habit pattern. Her perfectionism and shutting down emotional signals helped her to compensate for uncomfortable feelings of anxiety and frustration.

When she was a little girl, she learned that if she worked hard and excelled, she could dodge the seemingly relentless hovering of her worried parents. Her performance helped them relax and earned her the reward of freedom to do the things she wanted to do. Can you see how her behavior became reinforced? Expression of her feelings led to feeling smothered. Covering her anxiety led to compliments and freedom to do as she liked. The meaning she took with her into adulthood was "If I need others, they will smother me."

When What Once Worked Stops Working

Appearing competent and reserved also continued to work well for Nina in school and at work. But when she began her new job after a promotion, her habits weren't working so well. The most immediate problem Nina was facing was increased anxiety in social situations. Perfection may work great to manage familiar tasks and maintain status quo, but it can be a social killer!

People don't like you so much for what you do as for how you make them feel about themselves. And Nina's aloof perfectionism, although driven by her internal anxiety, was interpreted by her new colleagues as somewhat unfriendly. Her colleagues couldn't really connect and relate to her because of the veneer of competence she projected. This made them less friendly toward her and certainly less willing to give her the support she needed as she transitioned into her new role. Naturally, all of this contributed more to her social anxiety!

We develop our emotional habit patterns over time because, at some point, they totally worked to make us feel better or less bad, or to get our needs met. But they have an annoying tendency to stop working just when we're faced with a major life stressor or transition. And guess when you are faced with more stressors and transitions than any other time in your life? Yep, when you're just starting out! New schools, new jobs, new beaus, new apartments: everything is new and changing at this time in your life!

Transitions are inherently stressful because change pulls on our psychological resources. So our habits need to be updated. It's like when you go to your usual grocery store and it was remodeled, so now things aren't where you are used to finding them. How annoying is that? The first few times you go, you may find yourself automatically walking to the right where the produce used to be. But now you have to stop, pivot, and adapt. Now the produce is all the way on the left side of the store. You have to adapt to the new reality of your grocery store *context*. It's exactly like that in life. In life, however, the changes are happening constantly and more subtly. So we aren't as crystal clear on our need to stop, pivot, and adapt.

PAUSE. Can you identify some recent changes (or need for change) or stressful life situations you've been up against recently? Write these down in your journal to acknowledge the contextual factors that might be affecting you.

Since we're not as clear about the change in context, a lot of the time, we just notice that things aren't working the way we believe they "should" be. So what do we do when we're not making progress or are feeling like crap because we're not where we want to be? A lot of the time, we just try to double down on what used to work. Like mini-addictions, you may try to up the dosage of your *more better–less bad* habit in hopes it will work again. But at some point, you'll find that doing more of the same works less and less.

In fact, oftentimes, that thing you did, or way you thought, to solve the problem of vulnerability or discomfort becomes a new problem. Jessica's reassurance seeking worked at home, but in college, it was leading to more loneliness and isolation. Nina's perfectionism worked at school and for familiar tasks, but it made others less likely to approach her, only contributing to her social anxiety. Eddie's social avoidance and poor health habits worked in the very short term but compounded his depressive and anxiety symptoms. Are you getting the idea? This is how *the solution becomes the problem*.

In this book, you'll be learning about some common emotional habit patterns and how to identify your own. For now, the key takeaway is that the natural and automatic things we do to avoid, control, and minimize our emotional discomfort can become emotional habits that are like blind spots for us. They're reactive, automatic, and outside our awareness. But a good way to start getting a big-picture sense of how these day-to-day habit patterns show up is to look at two ends of a continuum in your personality.

The Personalities of the Overregulator and the Underregulator

We often hear people make global statements about personality. "Oh, that's just his personality," people say, as if personality is engraved in stone, immutable, and a done deal, like your eye color. But just as we now know that most genetically determined traits are influenced by life experiences and environmental factors, the same is true for personality.

Personality is defined as individual differences in characteristic *patterns* of thinking, feeling, and behaving. So, if our personality is the sum of our patterns and those patterns are the sum of our habits, then personality is, by definition, somewhat fluid. We can change our habit patterns! Sure, there is a set point from which you start. But your emotional habits are going to have a huge influence on the direction your personality and your life will take.

An important aspect of personality development is along a continuum between two poles (Luyten and Blatt 2013). As we're growing up, we're striving to find a balance in our identity needs. We're like Bambi trying to find what we stand for, our selfness. Along the way, we stumble from one extreme to the other. On one end of the continuum is our *interpersonal relatedness* need. We learn very quickly that to maintain good relations with others, we sometimes have to compromise and let go of our desires. The people around us, who support us and share our lives, are an essential part of our happiness. At the other end of the continuum is *self-definition*. Sometimes we need to set limits and disrupt others in the service of establishing a coherent and unique identity. Here, we need to assert our own needs first and set boundaries. Those psychological habits you've collected through childhood reflect your attempts to find a balance between these two poles.

Too much of either extreme can cause us to lose the flexible, adaptive responding we need to successfully negotiate our adult relationships, career goals, and freedoms we seek as a full-fledged emotional grown-up. You want to have some qualities of both and know which to rely on depending on the circumstances. These personality predispositions can underlie whether you tend to be an underregulator or an overregulator.

The Castle and the Village Metaphor

The castle and the village metaphor simplifies this theory so you can get a big-picture idea of how your habit patterns might be adding up, the benefits, and some of the costs. As you read this section, see if you can relate to one mode more than the other: Are you more like a castle person, an overregulator? Or more like a village person, an underregulator? This will give you a glimpse of what you'll be looking for throughout the book in your specific day-to-day emotional habit patterns. Imagine a world populated with small fiefdoms all throughout the land. Each has a castle, with a king or queen and villager dwellers.

Castle Dwellers

Castle dwellers live behind meticulously erected walls, high on a hill, outside of reach. The purpose of these walls, as with all good castles, is to present the appearance of security and superiority and to hide vulnerability. Castle folks invest a lot of time and energy in preserving this appearance of invincibility. In status, physically and financially, each success strengthens the walls of protection around them.

These walls are intended to protect the kings and queens from the messiness and dangers of those outside the walls. In people, this is analogous to the way many of us cope with (or fail to cope with) the vulnerable feelings of stress and strong emotions. This can be an extremely effective way of being in some situations. Like Nina, castle dwellers often appear to have it all together from the outside. They can garner respect and admiration and can often organize groups well and get others to lend a hand. In fact, this approach as self-protection is most effective in certain situations, such as when in a position of leadership or during a crisis. Sometimes erecting the castle wall is a healthy and positive thing to do to protect us from the infiltration of invaders.

"So?" you might say. "If it works, why not do it?" Here's the deal: As Nina learned, there are problems with this strategy of self-protection when it's rigidly relied upon. The primary cost of this pattern of coping is that it can create division and isolation. In some cases, the high and mighty walls become a source of anger or envy and can elicit attacks from outside. When these attacks come, castle folks hunker down and add another layer of protection. They pull up the bridges and shut the gates.

These extra-fortified walls can result in two common problems. The first problem is, as the walls get thicker and thicker so that castle folks may feel safer and safer, what do you think happens to their ability to see outside the walls? Over time, from behind the thick walls, the view of things outside gets narrowed and distorted. And thus, information to the contrary of what they saw before the walls went up doesn't get in. Do you see the problem here? As the world (or the context) outside the castle wall changes, which is inevitable, castle folks are protecting themselves based on old information. This is particularly problematic when castle dwellers are going through a life change or transition.

For Nina, her attempts to cling to the old habits of perfectionism and shutting down meant she wasn't responding to demands of the actual circumstances. Instead of engaging her new colleagues and appropriately asking for the help she needed, she was projecting unintended nonverbal messages of "stay away." Her habits were getting in the way of creative problem solving to get the support she needed at her new job, leading to her feeling more isolated and unsupported.

The second problem that emerges for castle dwellers is with their capacity to listen to and tolerate emotions, in themselves and others. Castle peeps often do an excellent job of keeping uncomfortable feelings and disturbing thoughts from their own awareness. But, as you will learn, our emotions provide guidance for what is deeply meaningful to us. Overuse of the castle defense (aka overregulation) can lead to lack of interest and a sense of not knowing what you truly desire. At the same time, these folks are mystified by the aggressions they elicit when they fail to relate to the expressed emotions of others. Castle folks can come across as fairly judgmental. The judgments are something like, "I've done such an excellent job at cutting off my messy emotions, so others should be able to do the same!" Emotions, difficult thoughts, and feelings are to be kept in control, under wraps, hidden. Empathy is difficult when we're in castle mode. Sooner or later, when the walls eventually become vulnerable under attack or criticism, castle folks have not had *practice* with feeling their own feelings. Thus, once penetrated, the walls can come crashing down in a full-blown emotional firestorm.

Village Dwellers

On the other hand, the folks in the village tend to be quite the opposite. Village dwellers have lots of experience feeling their feelings. These sensitive souls are the creative types, the artists, actors, writers, and such. They funnel their strong feelings into whatever it is they create in their lives, their work, their homes, and their loved ones. The villagers experience oodles of love *and* hate, and flourish when they have close intense relationships.

In fact, oftentimes, close connections are so essential to them that they can lose sight of what they truly desire. It's so distasteful to them to feel disconnected that their choices can become determined by whomever they are with. To maintain this sense of connection, village folks tend to put their own needs aside and often engage in overoffering. For the most part, they do this because they enjoy pleasing others and the feeling of connection due to their generosity. But when they feel disconnected or sense that others are coming to expect or take their kindness for granted, resentment and anger can build.

This is what Jessica was experiencing. Through the course of our work, Jessica discovered that she had a particularly difficult time coping when she didn't feel heard. As an exquisitely sensitive person, she picked up on even small slights. She perceived day-to-day conversations with new acquaintances as banal and annoying. It turned out that as a child, she felt that good behavior was ignored by her parents; meaningful attention was offered only when she had a crisis of some sort, which needed their assistance. The meaning Jessica internalized was that intense self-expression was essential to getting her needs met; it became her emotional habit.

Now, because the villagers do feel their feelings quite strongly, it's very difficult for them to not act on them. This was a difficulty Jessica frequently reported and explained why she would become paralyzed by her emotions. Contrary to the castle dwellers that block the influence of emotions on their perceptions, village folks tend to be run by their emotions. "If I feel it, it must be true!" is the belief here. You can see how this can lead to a lot of chaos and crises in the village.

Village relationships can have a lot of ups and downs, too. Villagers fight; they make up. They love, they hate, but these folks are authentic! It pains them to be otherwise. The problem for the sensitive and feeling villagers is that sometimes all the ups and downs and intensity of living in the village can become overwhelming. Their strong emotions can get the best of them and impact their ability to do the things they love: creating and connecting.

PAUSE. Which mode do you relate to most? Which qualities in the table below describe you? Tally up the totals in your journal to see which side you tend toward.

Table 1.1. *Two Poles of Emotional Habit Patterns*

Castle Mode (Overregulator)	Village Mode (Underregulator)
Cool	Warm
Logical	Emotional
Task oriented	Process oriented
Self-focused	Other focused
Low empathy	High empathy
Focused	Distracted
Poor "listening" to self	Poor "sitting" with self
Controlling	Laissez-faire
Perfectionistic	Artistic
Low creativity	High creativity
Overly rigid	Overly flexible
Tight boundaries	Flexible boundaries

The Costs of Living at the Extremes

Almost everyone can recognize themselves in either the castle dweller or the village dweller, or both. Sometimes, different situations bring out more of one mode versus the other. When we're in village mode, it's more difficult to "sit with" internal discomfort. Low tolerance for distress can make it very challenging to maintain commitments to long-term goals. Villagers experience strong, deep emotions on a more consistent basis. When emotions get strong, it's easy to lose focus and get lost in rumination and worries. Underregulation of emotions can result in chronic struggles with mood, anxiety, or behavioral problems.

On the other hand, as overregulators, castle folks have a harder time connecting with and "listening to" their emotions, needs, and desires. This can result in a lack of motivation, interest, vitality, and truly *knowing* what they care deeply about. There may be a heightened sense of threat and less sensitivity to reward, which contributes to over-control attempts (Lynch 2018). True dyed-in-the-wool castle dwellers often take longer to seek help. But when they do, it's usually because someone they care about insisted they do or their castle wall took a serious hit. Their difficulties tend to leak out as interpersonal disputes, sometimes related to anger management and very often as social anxiety. Ultimately, depression can result from pervasive feelings of loneliness and isolation.

Nina and Jessica demonstrate classic castle and village patterns respectively. Their descriptions are compilations of the patterns I have seen over and over again in my office. Research also describes possible predictors of these observations. Studies suggest that when parents emphasize conditional affection (based on performance), unhelpful castle traits of perfectionistic self-criticism and self-aggrandizing can take hold (Curran, Hill, and Williams 2017). On the other hand, two extremes of parental involvement have been related to more village traits: overfocus on solving problems and crises for children or, in contrast, failing to attend to or invalidating the child's internal feelings and emotions. The former may lead to later development of anxiety, depression, and lower life satisfaction and well-being (LeMoyne and Buchanan

2011; Nelson, Padilla-Walker, and Nielson 2015; Schiffrin et al. 2014). The latter has been related to lower distress tolerance and difficulties self-regulating emotions in relationships (Fruzzetti, Shenk, and Hoffman 2005; Sturrock and Mellor 2013).

Getting Unbound: Kicking Emotional Habits

Optimally, traits from each end of the pole are needed to be most effective in managing emotions in pursuit of our goals, depending on the situation. Sometimes it's most effective to raise the castle wall to protect yourself, maintain your independence, and thus endure feelings of disconnection and isolation. Sometimes it's most effective to feel the discomfort of vulnerability in the service of connecting and creating with others. The *key* to successfully transitioning into and throughout adulthood is to learn how to skillfully and flexibly adopt what works in a particular context.

In the chapters that follow, I will guide you on your path of self-discovery. Each chapter will add a layer to your self-understanding and offer you a road map to building the story of your life, as you want it to read. Like all great excursions, there will be moments of awe and glory as well as dread, boredom, and frustration. But what's the alternative? More of the same? Come: take these words as breadcrumbs along your path toward mastering adulthood.

CHAPTER 2

Your Mind-Body Vehicle: Your Holistic System

If a butterfly flaps its wings in New Mexico,
We may see a hurricane in China.

—The Butterfly Effect, from the
chaos theory of mathematics

It's all connected, people!

Everything has a cause. What those causes are can't always be known. Nonetheless, whether the cause is near or far, everything is connected. When you are late for a meeting, there is a cause. When relationships are rocky, there is a cause. When you're stuck in a funk and can't pull out, there is a cause. And when you just can't seem to get traction figuring out and moving toward your goals...yep, there is always a cause.

The good news is that, with the tools and skills you'll be learning, you'll be able to start hacking into the system that underlies your behavior, identify your emotional habits, and demystify some of those causes—the ones that are in your sphere of control! Of course, there will always be stuff that's outside your control; that's just part of life. And still, as the Greek philosopher Epictetus said, "It is not what happens to you, but how you react to it that matters."

So, the very first step to empowering yourself to master this thing called adulthood is understanding the system of interrelated parts—the hardwiring in all humans—that underlies the emotional habits you get stuck in. Whether you identified more as a castle or a village person in the last chapter, knowing the basic mechanics of how your holistic system operates will empower you to make the change you want in your life. This chapter will help you understand the components of your internal reactions, which make up the missing links between stimulus and response, cause and effect. With this info in hand, you'll later be able to see how your unique story gets plugged into the system and the places you might be getting stuck!

Getting to Know Your Mind-Body Vehicle

A good way to think about the complex interaction between your happiness and your life is to think of your mind-body as a vehicle in which you drive the roads of life. That body in which you are sitting, right now, reading these words is your vehicle—and has been from the day you were born, through elementary, middle, and high school until now. In it, you have traveled all the roads of your life to get to this precise moment. It's the vehicle through which you perceive and experience the road of life as either comfortable or uncomfortable.

There are, of course, lots of different kinds of vehicles, in different sizes, colors, makes, and models. Some are more hardy, like an SUV, and can haul the heavy loads and take the bumps in life pretty well but might not have a lot of pickup or have a few blind spots. Others may be sportier and can zip around but don't go off-road so well and maybe need a bit more maintenance. Each of us is a unique type of vehicle, which comprises all kinds of different strengths and vulnerabilities.

PAUSE. What type of vehicle might you inhabit? Describe it in your journal. Is your vehicle durable or delicate? Similar to others on the road or different? A bright attention-getting color or more subtle? What are your vehicle's specific strengths and vulnerabilities?

Notice if your mind starts churning out opinions about the type of mind-body vehicle you inhabit. When you begin this work and reflect on your body, it's easy to get swept away by thoughts and opinions about the machine you inhabit. It might also be challenging for you to attend to your physical being if your body has been in a place of former trauma or is currently a source of discomfort. For now, I invite you to simply consider your body as your vehicle of transportation. And ask yourself this question: Is it "better" to drive an SUV or a sports car? You may hold a strong opinion or belief about the answer to this question. But the fact is, an SUV is no better or worse than a sports car; it depends upon the demands of the road from moment to moment.

It's the fit between the demands of the road and the vehicle that *in part* determines the comfort or discomfort you experience in any given moment. But the vehicle (or your biology) is only one component contributing to how you feel and how successfully you get where you want to go. Equally important, and the essential takeaway here, is paying attention to how well the vehicle is taken care of and the skillfulness of the driver. Unlike a real car, you can't turn this one in for a new one. It's the only one you've got, so caring for it is key! This book is about taking care of the vehicle you live in and getting you pointed in the direction that brings joy and meaning to your life. The mindfulness and self-care skills you'll learn will help you optimize the performance of that awesome machine you live in!

PAUSE. Right now, as you read the words on this page, can you notice that there is a *you* there seeing, from behind your own eyes, behind your own face, the words on this page? Can you notice that you feel certain physical sensations of pressure, temperature, and touch? Notice the weight of this book, Kindle, or iPad. As you look, from behind your own eyes, behind your own face, you are looking out from inside your own vehicle. Who's noticing? Who is the driver?

Good noticing! After reading the Pause practice, did you get the felt sense of this metaphor? Did it become clearer that you are neither your vehicle (your body) nor your internal experiences (your mind)? There is a *you* there who can mindfully reflect on the experiences your mind and body produce. So, if you can reflect on these experiences, there is a part of you, a conscious part, that is beyond those thoughts and feelings. Make sense? You are the driver!

Moving beyond emotional habits is about taking ahold of the steering wheel to move that vehicle of yours where you want to go! It's about homing in on what's important to you and building the skills you need to manage the inevitable discomfort that comes up along the way. Sure, we can all get pulled into our repertoires of reactivity as if we *are* those experiences. "That's just who I am," or "who they are," we often hear people say. It's as if we literally believe we *are* our experiences. But as you just saw for yourself, we have a unique ability as conscious humans to step back, to get some space in our awareness, and to observe our experience. That *observer* part of you is always there. Actually, if there is a place that is really you, a kind of soul place, I would say the observer place is it!

That's who you want calling the shots in your adulting endeavors, not some worn-out, old autopilot emotional habits that might have worked once or may get you through difficulties but are now distracting you from your authentic path. As the driver, sometimes the roads you have to travel won't match the strengths of your vehicle. That means the tasks you have to tackle will be harder for you than for others who have a different type of vehicle. And sometimes you will be fortunate, and the road will be smoother riding for you than for others. Life's not always fair that way. But it's from this space of *ownership*, rather than reactivity, that you can learn to more skillfully negotiate the bumpy terrain of life.

User's Manual 101

Regardless of what type of vehicle you inhabit, there's a standard-issue system of interrelated parts that underlies your enjoyment of the ride. Just like your car, each part has particular needs for its maintenance. So it's worth taking a minute to learn about what's going on under the hood of your vehicle so that when it's having issues, you know where to check for the source of the problem.

All cars share the same primary components: an engine, a steering wheel, and tires, which influence the comfort of the ride inside the vehicle. Similarly, all humans share a system of parts that make our psyche tick and influence our day-to-day moods and motivation. We process and perceive the facts outside the vehicle through the *emotions*, *thoughts*, and *action impulses* (ETA) we feel inside the vehicle.

This mind matrix, which I call the *ETA regulator* (a handy mnemonic to remember the components), works seamlessly in the background to create our perception (our happiness or discontent) of the facts in our lives. Understanding how each component contributes to your holistic system is the first step to later being able to more mindfully use your skills to make adjustments when you need to up- or downregulate.

IF **EMOTIONS** ARE THE ENGINE,
THOUGHTS ARE THE STEERING,
AND **ACTIONS** ARE THE TIRES,

Emotions: The Engine That Drives Us

We humans have a rather conflicted relationship with our emotions. We all want more of the good ones, like joy, inspiration, awe, and love. But we do our best to avoid the uncomfortable ones, like sadness, disappointment, anxiety, and (heaven forbid) shame. Heck, it was probably how you were raised. Can I see a show of hands of those who heard the proverbial, "I just want you to be happy, Honey," from Mom and Dad? It's true, right? That's probably part of the reason you picked up this book. You were told you're supposed to be happy!

Of course, your parents had the best of intentions encouraging you toward happiness. That's still a great goal! It was the "just" part that might have thrown a monkey wrench into things. Well, what my generation and those before didn't know, but you guys can pass on to your kids, is this: Just as we can't cut part of the engine in a car without shutting down the whole thing, we can't shut off some emotions without dimming all of them. Our mind-body vehicle simply wasn't designed with a kill switch for certain feelings. It doesn't work.

PAUSE. Try this experiment. Right now, as you read these words, move your attention to feel your butt in the chair you are sitting in (or some other very tangible sensation). Okay, feel your butt? Got buttness? Good! The sensations were there all along, but you just moved your attention to bring these physical feelings into awareness. Now, try this. Try to *unfeel* your butt. Just stop feeling it. Go ahead, I'll wait.

Any luck trying to *not* feel something (your butt in this case) once it was in awareness? Of course not! When we feel something, we cannot simply *unfeel* it! Yet, so often we try to do this with our emotional feelings. We may have limited success by bringing something different to mind. Distraction works pretty darn well, for a little while. But what do you think happens to your focus muscles when you've overrelied on distraction as a habit to reduce discomfort? What you probably noticed is that the more you try to unfeel your butt, the *more* you feel it!

Something similar happens when we try to not feel our emotions. The more we try to get rid of them, the more we tend to get stuck in them. This is because our emotions serve an essential function, not only for our survival, but also in pursuing the things that matter to us.

The Purpose of Emotions

Can you remember the last time you felt the *full-body sensory* experience of your emotions? The burning tears and hot face of sadness, the pounding chest and sweaty palms of anxiety, the narrowed eyes and tensed muscles of anger, or the tender open arms and soft lips of love? Those delightfully infuriating cascades can send us into our own virtual reality, which can be exhilarating or terrifying. But without them, we wouldn't have the drive we need—to hunt, to care, to create, and to connect.

The embodied experience of our emotions has guaranteed the survival of human beings and our success as a species. Think about it for a second. What would've happened if early humans didn't have emotions? Let's take fear for a straightforward example. Say you're an early human, out for a day of hunting. You're meandering along through the bushes and…suddenly, you hear a snap of a branch behind you, feel hot breath on your neck, and finally hear the deep rumbling of a growl. What would happen if you were purely logical—had no emotion—as you calmly contemplated your next move?

YOU WOULD DIE!

When our ancestors were struggling to stay alive so they could live long enough to pass their genes on to the next generation, they had to act and react super fast to not get killed by a saber-tooth tiger or some other dire threat. Right? This is the basic premise of evolution: stay alive and pass on your genes—survival of the fittest. Our most basic internal motivation comes from our emotions!

In many ways, the modern age and all of its conveniences have unintentionally sanitized us from our deepest natures—the convenience of a pill for every pain, endless distractions from the torments of reality, or an app (or Mom) to solve every problem has minimized our need, and thus our ability, to turn inward and listen to the meaningful messages of our emotions. Above and beyond the animal drives for survival, emotions are also our guideposts for our deepest yearnings as conscious beings. There are three basic communication functions of emotions.

Emotions Communicate to Others

Imagine a friend comes to you to share something meaningful and important. How do you imagine this scene? Perhaps you see her leaning in toward you with a furrowed brow, eyes moist from tears, and her voice tone or tempo different from usual. All of these "affective cues" bid you to pay closer attention. Even if she said nothing, these emotional cues are more powerful than her words.

Conversely, what if it was you seeking a friend's support, and you are met with no emotional expression? You will likely feel less understood than if he matched your tone and expression. It's in the vulnerable space of emotional communications that we connect—through empathy. Expressions of our primary emotions are preverbal, universal, and cross-cultural. No one had to teach you that a smile means someone is happy or tears mean someone is unhappy. So our expressions bring us together across the barriers of language. Think back to what was happening with Nina. In blocking her emotional signals, others didn't relate to her or offer her the support she so eagerly wanted. When we close off our emotions, we lose an essential piece of the communication and the connection.

Emotions Motivate Action Impulses

Above and beyond the proverbial fight, flight, or freeze reaction, each emotion compels a particular action tendency. The biological underpinnings of emotions convey fast-acting yet subtle bodily sensations, which we experience as impulses to take a necessary action to get our needs met. Sadness motivates us to withdraw and heal, fear tells us to run away or avoid, anger compels us to get larger and louder to fight an injustice or protect a boundary, and guilt motivates us to make amends. Lastly, what do you think would happen to all of those screaming, crying, pooping little people without love? You can find a handy table summarizing the Functions of Primary Emotions at http://www .newharbinger.com/41931. The point here is that when we disconnect from our primary emotions, we lose our drive and motivation to take the needed actions and pursue our deepest desires.

PAUSE. Is lack of motivation one of the reasons you picked up this book?

Emotions Signal Our Deepest Needs

"We hurt where we care. We care where we hurt," says Steven Hayes, PhD, the developer of acceptance and commitment therapy (ACT), in his inspiring TED Talk (2016). Emotions send us important messages about the things we really care about. Each is informing us of what it is we value and hold dear. When we disconnect from them, we risk muting the awareness of what's important to us. This is an essential takeaway because only you can surmise what is truly important to you. You simply cannot Google the answer to, "What is my authentic calling?" When you learn to truly listen to your primary emotions, you are listening for clues to your deeper callings, your purpose, and the direction you want your life to take.

PAUSE. Take a look at the Functions of Primary Emotions table. Which emotions do you wish you could get rid of? Now that you know their purpose, would you really want to get rid of them entirely? What might be the cost of doing so? Journal a bit about your answer.

"Dirty Emotions": the Red Herring

I'm guessing right about now you may be thinking, *Yeah, not my problem. I'm super aware of my emotions! That's why I bought this darned book!* I hear you. And for all my village dwellers out there, I believe you. Sometimes, you are too aware of your emotions! My question for you is this: Which emotions are you aware of?

Gavin came to me seeking skills to cope with the depression he had been struggling with since childhood. He had been in traditional therapy for several years, working through the emotional abuse and neglect by his alcoholic parents. But while doing the same work you'll be doing here, he found that his sadness was actually the secondary (possibly even the tertiary) emotion. In other words, he was having emotions about his emotions.

Gavin's past experience with his highly volatile family made it impossible for him to assert his own needs without being ridiculed or punished in some way. So naturally, the belief "Having needs that differ from others is dangerous" was programmed in him. In the image below, you can see how the bidirectional arrows in Gavin's ETA regulator got programmed. Initial feelings of anger immediately led to the old assumption that he was powerless. He became highly anxious whenever he would feel even a hint of anger. Thus, instead of connecting with the

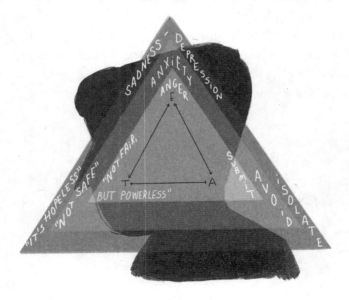

more natural emotion associated with "not fair," which is anger, he associated differences in needs with powerlessness and anxiety.

The action impulse that goes with anxiety is to run away or avoid. Over time, because of his emotional habit pattern of avoidance, Gavin was collecting more and more experiences that confirmed his power-lessness beliefs. Because anger made him anxious, he was avoiding, rather than asserting himself when appropriate. Naturally, his avoid-ance only served to increase his sadness, frustration, and sense of pow-erlessness because he never had the opportunity to experience a different outcome. Once he discovered that anger was actually a justi-fied primary emotion, he learned the same skills you will learn for healthy and effective assertiveness and regulating anxiety. Once he mastered these skills, his depressive symptoms remitted.

Emotions become extra confusing when we have secondary emo-tions, or an emotion about an emotion, because they send an ineffective message. Sometimes these sequences are called secondary emotions or "dirty emotions"—"dirty" because they don't hold the same clean com-munication value as the authentic primary emotion. The important thing to remember is that the secondary emotions are like a red herring. They distract us (and thus protect us) from the more vulnerable feelings of the primary emotion. But ultimately, they lead us astray because they activate an inaccurate message, to ourselves and to others.

PAUSE. Consider this: if you're sad because of a loss or disappointment but express emotions of anger, will you get the needs of sadness (which are healing and empathy) or the needs of anger (which say, "Get away from me") met?

Over time, if we have a bunch of experiences in which emotions lead to unpleasant outcomes, we can actually become somewhat "emotion phobic," just like you can become afraid of dogs if you were bitten as a child. After repeated negative experiences with our emo-tions, we come to the natural (but unhelpful) conclusion that emotions lead to bad things, are a threat, and should be hidden, gotten rid of, or suppressed. The more bad experiences we have with our emotions, the more we rely on our emotional habits to avoid feeling them, the further we get from the important messages they hold, and the more entangled we become in whatever the habit is!

PAUSE. Have you had past experiences in which strong emotions (in yourself or others) led to negative outcomes? What beliefs do you now hold about emotions? Write a bit about these memories in your journal.

Like Gavin, you will learn how to tell the difference between the helpful emotions, which can guide you toward the things you care about, and the red herrings that take you off track. The skills you will be learning will help you build a better relationship with your primary informative emotions so that the dirty emotions don't hijack your observer and lead you astray!

Thoughts: The Augmented Reality Your Mind Creates

In the movie *Divergent*, the main character Tris is subjected to a virtual reality test to assess how she copes with fear. Her test culminates in a virtual black room where she's trapped in a glass box that quickly begins flooding with water. She screeches in fear as she bangs on the glass, "Hey! Help me!" She pounds and kicks the glass as her fight-or-flight reaction to fear kicks in. The water fills to the top of the glass box, and all becomes still. We see Tris slow down, things become quiet, and she enters observer mode. She slowly taps the glass with her index finger very deliberately as she says, "This isn't real." The glass cracks and then shatters. She spills out, escaping the confines of the box. And of course, she passes the test.

Our mind creates an augmented reality, not too dissimilar to Tris's virtual reality experience. The thoughts we have can actually activate our brain as if the things we are thinking about are real, not just imagined. Whether you're fantasizing about an amazing date with a recent crush or imagining why he or she hasn't replied right away to your text, you live that thought as if it were true! Two ways our mind can trap us in this virtual reality are assumption land and sticky thoughts.

PAUSE. What's your favorite flavor of ice cream? Cup or cone? Toppings? Imagine that first perfect bite or lick. Imagine how it tastes, the sensations of cold as it melts to that just-right consistency. What do you notice? Did your mouth water? Are you wondering if there is any ice cream in the freezer or if you should take action to go get some? Why are you reacting like that? There's no ice cream here. It's just your augmented reality maker!

Assumption Land: When Thoughts Live Outside Awareness

In Buddhism, there's an ancient parable about six blind men who are asked to describe an elephant. The six men surround the elephant, and each describes his perception from his limited worldview.

"This is a beast that is a massive wall of rough texture," says the first blind man.

"On the contrary," says the second. "Here is a long, smooth creature with a bit of fluff at the end," says the man at the tail end of the elephant.

"Don't be a fool!" says the third blind man. "This is four separate column-shaped animals."

You get the idea. I don't care how well traveled you are or how much you've seen—your worldview is limited. Everyone's worldview is limited. But we still get vehement about our position of being "right," which just entrenches us in the rigidity of our ETA system and emotional habit patterns.

PAUSE. As a seeker, are you willing to begin opening up to your own blind spots and what you might be missing?

We humans just eat up a good story! This ability to use our visual and verbal stories in our mind makes us uniquely able to learn from the stories of our tribes and our culture. We don't actually have to live every experience to learn from it. Unfortunately, our creative storytelling mind can also work against us. The problem is, once a belief is in there good and solid, like a habit, it can shift from the conscious place to the assumption place. Once thoughts and ideas retire in assumption land, it's really hard to see evidence to the contrary, evidence that might disconfirm the story we're holding on to (and help us grow past the suffering we get stuck in).

The stories we collect from experience and our tribe become tacit assumptions or unconscious *rules* about how the world works. We often hear people say, "That's just how I was raised." Jessica assumed that others *should* help her manage her fears and anxiety. Nina assumed that if she asked others for help, she would be smothered with unhelpful attention. Both made natural assumptions from their past experiences but failed to gather new information.

PAUSE. Since we *all* make assumptions, you do it too. Can you identify some common rules of your culture that are taken as absolute facts? Consider how someone from another culture might see them.

Sticky Thoughts: How Emotions Mess Up Thinking

We all like to think we're open-minded of course. But when you throw an emotion in there to fuel a belief, man oh man, can those beliefs get impenetrable! That's because how we feel is like fuel for how we think. Our thoughts, particularly ones that evoke strong emotions, get sticky.

Tris knew she was in a virtual reality test when she went in. But when the panic set in, she forgot as her mind and body started to react to the mounting waterline. This happens. Many classic studies have shown that, even when we are told a situation is not real, our emotional reactions can take over, and we forget! Logic and reason are no longer accessible.

Our emotional state at any given moment is like wearing tinted glasses. Just as blue lenses will make it difficult to see green and red and will highlight similar colors, such as purple, when we're sad, angry, or anxious, we have what is called a *negativity bias*. We feel a particular way, so it's as if we look around to find a reason we feel that way. I'm guessing you know this from your own experience. You know, that time when you were so absolutely and completely sure you *knew* that X, Y, or Z was happening, going to happen, or not going to happen? Remember that time? And then you were wrong? Yeah, that's what our mind can deceive us with when we have strong emotions and beliefs.

Actions: Your Most Powerful Ally

As a behavioral psychologist, I get really geeked out about the power of our actions to impact our mental health. That's because our actions— the things we do with our feet, hands, and voice—are the only things truly in our control. No prescription needed. (Side effects may include increased sense of empowerment, independence, and freedom from the tyranny of our emotions.) Everything from small changes in facial expression and body posture to our daily health habits and big-picture choices can have powerful and even biological impacts on our mental health.

It's easy to overlook the impact because each action we take is like a pebble on the beach of our life. Sometimes we can clearly see the contribution of a choice on the landscape of our happiness. But more often, it's the accumulation of many, many small acts over time that build the beach of the life we want, or don't want.

PAUSE. Try this experiment for yourself to feel how small actions can influence your mood state. Right now, with your body and facial expression, playact sadness: slump down a bit, allow the corners of your mouth to curve down, and maybe furrow your brow. Take a mental snapshot of how you feel. Now, shift your body posture to a dignified, upright position, drop your shoulders down and back, open your eyes a bit wider, and slowly, gently (not forcing) allow the corners of your mouth to float up. Take a mental snapshot of how you feel.

You likely noticed what researchers have found (Draft and Pressman 2012): simple changes in our actions, body posture, and facial expressions can add a pebble to the beach of our happiness. This is just a small example of the awesome power your actions can have on your mood. Because of that powerful, bidirectional emotion-action interaction, your actions are going to be your most powerful tool. In other words, just as your emotions push for certain behaviors, certain behaviors push for certain emotions.

Taking Control of the Vehicle

It gets tricky though, because the tide of our emotions can be pretty strong, and we can honestly *feel* out of control! Because emotions are carrying that message, it just won't *feel* right to do something different than what your emotions are telling you to do. It will *feel* fake or inauthentic to take an action that doesn't correspond to the emotion.

So the most challenging part of being skillful, and one of the first things I tell people when they come to see me, is this:

When emotions are strong, and you really, really need to use your skills, you totally won't want to!

Another reason behavior change can be tough is because your mind jumps in there as well to egg you on: *It'll be fine. Just this once is okay.* Two thoughts that show up again and again are, *I shouldn't have to make all this effort (to override my autopilot)!* and *It's too hard!* Yeah, I hear you! While the skills you are learning in this book are pretty simple, overriding the well-practiced autopilot can be tough. So, like learning any new skill, it's going to take a fair degree of practice and commitment.

Making a Commitment to Practice

We become what we practice. At the end of the day, the adult you become will be dictated by the sum total of all the large and small actions you take during this incarnation. So, sorry to say, you will not be remembered for all those genius creative thoughts you think, the deep emotions you feel, or even the observer you. The statement you make in this lifetime is made in your actions.

To reconcile this dilemma between doing what *feels* right and what works to leave your mark beyond adulting, it's important to know why the change you seek matters to *you.* As you move through the pages that follow—seeking, learning, and growing—your commitment may get wobbly from time to time. That's normal. When it does, the trick is to reconnect the engine: remember why you care! Take a moment to rev up your commitment by answering the following questions in your journal. If you ever start feeling pessimistic or notice you're avoiding commitment, go back to that page and remind yourself why this work is for *you* (not for me, your parents, or anyone else).

PAUSE. If this book were magic, what changes would you like it to help you make? What do you think is the biggest barrier to achieving those changes? Why is it important for you to overcome the barriers and make the changes you can? In ten years, what would you like your best friends, partner, or colleagues to say about your courage and commitment?

CHAPTER 3

Passengers:
The Hijackers and Bullies

Life is difficult. This is a great truth, one of the greatest truths. It is a great truth because once we truly see this truth, we transcend it.

> —M. Scott Peck, *The Road Less Traveled:*
> *A New Psychology of Love, Traditional*
> *Values, and Spiritual Growth*

"You're disrespecting me!" Amy asserted in a louder-than-normal sharp tone one Thursday evening in my office. "You don't get it," she went on. "Without me, that department would be a joke! And it's just inappropriate for you to question that." Clearly, I had hit a nerve. "Oh gosh, I'm sorry, Amy. I can see my confusion about your position at work is upsetting you," I said, aiming to validate her feelings so we could communicate more effectively. "Help me understand what I'm missing." I continued to inquire because people yell only when they don't feel heard. I was diving in to do my best to hear what was happening inside Amy.

I was genuinely confused because when we first began working together, Amy was super excited when she told me she had just gotten a job as an admin assistant. As a first job, it was a great opportunity for her to learn the ropes in an industry in which she was interested. Now she was expressing a lot of anger that the more senior employees were complaining to her boss about Amy's interpersonal style. They too were "disrespecting" her. I was wondering if something else was going on. Could the anger and irritability really be a red-herring emotion for something even more painful underneath?

"I know they've been there way longer than I have," she conceded. "I get it. But it's my job to keep that place running. They need to understand!"

"Oh," I replied with genuine interest. "I see my confusion; I was under the impression that you were the assistant to the guy who kept the place running. Am I mistaken?"

The tone of her voice was even more forceful now, "That's just a title! I'm not *just* an assistant who gets coffee and answers the phone."

And there it was! Somewhere between the craving and clinging to the feeling of being respected and the pushing away of being *just* an assistant was a place Amy didn't want to go: a vulnerable place, which she was protecting by pushing me away with her anger. Her unusually strong reaction to my failure to see her as "more than *just* an assistant" seemed like a sure sign. We were dealing with a *passenger*.

Passengers are our sensitive spots of thinking and feeling that can hide just outside awareness—until we stumble upon something that triggers them. Those vulnerable spots show up as constellations of internal reactions (emotions, thoughts, and sensations) that can cause us to react in ways that are ineffective and add unnecessary suffering to our lives.

Passengers: The Stuff We Bring with Us

From the moment your mind-body vehicle set out on the road of life, you started collecting them. Passengers enter our psyche from the roads we travel: our families, the situations and people we encounter, and factual events, which everyone would agree occurred. Over time, we internalize our *perceptions* of these events as passengers on board our mind-body vehicle. All the good days and bad days, special days, and everyday events add to the roster of passengers. Passengers are the residue of past experiences that we carry within us and often superimpose, like a veil, over the facts in the present moment. (So no, your ex is not a passenger. He is a fact on the road; people are not passengers.)

You really notice them when you stumble upon something that reminds you of an early hurt or vulnerability. In middle school, Amy had some really tough experiences with being bullied. Those incidents caused unbearable feelings of powerlessness and shame at the time. So for her, those two feeling passengers tended to hang out together. When she started her new job, she was by definition in the less powerful position. As a result, the regular everyday feelings associated with being new on the job, which required her to be deferential to those with more experience, were triggering the older feelings—her passengers.

Our passengers are those tender spots of feelings and beliefs that push us around to do all kinds of stuff we wouldn't otherwise do. They are the trigger-related reactions we have *inside* our skin: the sensations, perceptions, beliefs, and emotions. They're there where you find your pet peeves—the stuff that makes you go apeshit, bugs the snot out of you, or just knocks you off your game. They also make you ramp up those defensive emotional habits. If you notice strong reactions to stuff other people take in stride, yep, that's a passenger.

They are a part of you, but not you. Remember the observer place? As the observer, you are aware of your internal experience, but not the same as it. You are the conscious container of those thoughts and feelings. From that place, you can start to see those old passengers for what they are: a symphony of internal reactions, based on old programming. These guys can be super distracting and demanding, sometimes making it really hard to go where you want to go. But they cannot drive your vehicle! Only you are in control of your decisions and taking the actions needed to get there.

PAUSE. What are some key memories in your life that might have landed some passengers on board your vehicle? Consider any old hurts or stressful times in your past. Write a few lines about these memories, and the specific emotions they elicited, in your journal.

Passenger Warning Signs

Passengers underlie the emotional habits we've developed to keep uncomfortable thoughts and feelings outside our awareness. So it can take some time to identify who's on board and make the connection to the resulting mayhem. Even so, there were a couple of clues that helped Amy recognize that she was having a passenger reaction. From the exercises she had been practicing, and you will be learning in coming chapters, Amy was able to step back just enough to see that there was a whiff of a familiar pattern.

First, she recognized that there had been several other situations that triggered the thought that she was being disrespected, which led to feelings of anger. The pattern here was that it was coming from more than one source. When something seems to be happening over and over again in our life, the common denominator is often a passenger. Sometimes she could white-knuckle her way through these emotions. But other times, Amy's actions (tone of voice, speech pattern, or overasserting herself) gave her away—thus, the complaints from her fellow employees.

Actually, anger is the justified emotion when someone is truly overstepping a boundary. But the second clue was that Amy was having a more elevated reaction than would be anticipated for the facts of the situation. A normal reaction becomes heightened when there's a passenger involved because we're reacting to the added pain of an old hurt, not just what is happening in the moment.

PAUSE. Do you notice any particular situations that trigger stronger-than-needed reactions or repeated patterns in your life that might be passenger driven?

The passenger metaphor (adapted from Hayes, Strosahl, and Wilson 1999) illustrates what psychologists call the *biopsychosocial theory* of mental health: The interaction between our biology (our vehicle), psychology (passengers), and social landscape (the road) is what produces, and constantly influences, the status of our mental health and how well we are coping. Let's explore some of the unique road conditions that have influenced your generation, the passengers, and autopilot emotional habits that tend to come up.

Road Conditions in the Millennial Age

Naturally, our cultural and social upbringing is going to have an important influence on our passenger list. We need look no further than the people we know and encounter from diverse backgrounds to see this! If you grew up with an intact family that loved and adored you, your passengers will be very different from someone who did not. And if you were of the predominant race and religion in your neighborhood, your experience of the world is also much different than someone who was not. So, just as different situations influence our views of the world, so too does the time in which we were born. There are some key events you may have experienced growing up in the 1990s and early 2000s that may influence your passenger struggles.

There's definitely no one-size-fits-all when looking for passengers and emotional habit patterns. The number of different permutations of how the facts on the road intersect with the strengths and vulnerabilities of your vehicle to produce the passenger list is infinite! If you're anything like the countless young adults I've known, taught, and worked with, then you can't be boxed into the grand overgeneralizations we've seen in the media in recent years. We've all heard the disparaging labels (narcissistic, lazy, entitled, and so forth) given to twenty-somethings in recent years. Those labels clearly fail to account for the very real road conditions that you've had to navigate and that naturally shaped the ways you think, feel, and react to certain situations in your life.

More Options: The Tyranny of Choice

The road condition. With science to help extend fertility, the average age for getting married and starting a family is getting later and later. Many young adults are choosing to bypass traditional markers of adulthood altogether. Today, you have more time to mature, experiment, and find your true calling. This period of "emerging adulthood" is when you get to explore who you are and what you want (Arnett 2004). Your career path is open and yours for the making as new technologies lead to new opportunities.

The passengers. At the intersection of infinite possibilities and searching for your true calling are more anxiety and insecurity passengers.

The stats are real! More twenty-somethings are reporting symptoms of anxiety and stress, particularly related to financial security, the political climate, and mental and reproductive health care, than any other generation (American Psychological Association 2017, 2018). Changes in jobs, partners, and living conditions are also much more common (LinkedIn 2017), which means your mind-body vehicle has to be extra flexible and adaptive. You've inherited the "tyranny of choice" problem. In a world where anything is possible—*Crap! Anything is possible!*—decision making can become overwhelming!

The autopilot reactivity. Whereas prior generations have gotten stuck in *midlife* crises from the oppressive predictability, the abundance of choices today is creating the proverbial *quarter-life* crisis: debilitating feelings of uncertainty (Osborn 2017)! Uncertainty is a normal part of life, particularly when you're just starting out as an adult. But recent studies have identified specific difficulties with uncertainty, known as "uncertainty intolerance" (UI), as a strong underlying predictor of numerous anxiety, depressive, and even eating disorders (Carleton 2016). According to R. Nicholas Carleton (2018), a predominant researcher of UI, "Millennials may indeed be having more difficulties with uncertainty than previous generations."

The natural reaction to anxiety is to try to avoid or control it. When you see someone who is avoiding or controlling, you know there's an anxiety passenger on board! As the most educated generation in history, perfectionistic patterns of coping with anxiety are on the rise. There are three common unhelpful patterns of perfectionism: *pushing through*, which frequently leads to irritability and burnout; *avoidance of responsibility*, due to a related belief that "anything less than perfect is failure"; and *procrastination*, which leads to less productive, rushed performance (Crosby et al. 2013). In fact, your generation is also reporting more reliance on passive ways of avoiding. And of course you are! There are so many great ways to avoid stress now, from binge-watching to home delivery of your favorite food, drink, or bud. It's just so easy to fill our days with feel-good-now-pay-later activities.

PAUSE. Is the uncertainty passenger (or any of its crew: anxiety, worry, fear, agitation) causing mayhem on your vehicle? What are some things you do or ways you think to try to avoid or control uncertainty or anxiety?

More Access: Social Media Mayhem

The road condition. Thanks to social media and the Internet, it's easier now than ever to envision innovative and creative ways of solving problems. The barriers to access to others for support and collaboration have all but been eradicated. You can literally start your own media channel on YouTube. You can crowdsource ideas and expertise from collaborators around the globe. But it's also well known that the social media programmers have tapped into the science of behaviorism and our basic human need to connect to get you hooked on checking and posting (Veissière and Stendel 2018). The rewarding properties of likes, clicks, and shares get us hooked, like a quick high.

The passengers. Screen crawling pulls all of us into unproductive distraction and can create deficits in our attention muscles. Research is beginning to show that more screen time can lead to difficulty in our ability to hold attention if there's no immediate reward (Swing et al. 2010). Screen time in youth actually correlates with later development of an ADHD diagnosis. Today, it's harder and harder to hold steady attention. With all the easy access, our mind insists "Things *should* go faster!" and "This *should* be easier!" The frustration and boredom passengers might be ever present—cajoling less-than-helpful emotional habits of Internet surfing to keep them quiet.

Social networking can also quickly shift to social comparisons. "Am I up, or am I down?" judgments can send your mood all over the place. Interestingly, it's long been understood by psychologists that we humans are compelled to make social comparisons (Festinger 1954). Particularly when there is no objective measure of success, we will look to those we see around us. Loads of research are showing that when we turn to social media too often, we feel worse (for example, Lin et al.

2016; Primack et al. 2017; Ulz, Muscanell, and Cameran 2015). Time dedicated to social media correlates with increases in all kinds of tough passengers. Check your own experience. Have you noticed that the jealousy (particularly on Snapchat), loneliness, and body-judging passengers (Fardouly et al. 2015) show up when you're cruising your friends' (or worse, your ex's) page late at night?

The autopilot reactivity. It has long been known that performing in front of a group (which is what it can feel like when posting your life on social media) can either facilitate or inhibit performance. When we are already skilled at a task, group presence tends to improve performance. As one castle client once said to me, "If you didn't post it, it's like it didn't happen!" Our choices may become more influenced by the selfie opportunity than by what is truly meaningful. On the other hand, when we're novices (as when we first begin adulting), we naturally become more inhibited when observed by others (Markus 1978). So much access to the perfectly curated images of our "friends" compels us into our natural upward or downward judgments. The performance quality of social engagement may start to lead to more self-judgment, avoidance, and paradoxically, more isolation.

PAUSE. Is social media an emotional habit you use to distract yourself from difficult passenger feelings? Or does it bring passengers up for you? What do you notice in your thinking and emotions when you use social media?

More Support: Less Independence

The road condition. Parenting styles have also changed a ton in the past few decades! According to the Pew Research Center (Parker and Livingston 2014), the amount of time fathers spend with their children has tripled, and mothers have increased attendance by 60 percent. That might be part of the reason most young adults today say they're very close to their family and consider their parents more like close friends than authority figures. Perhaps you too are in daily contact with your parents (often multiple times per day) via text messaging, seeking guidance or support. Quite possibly, you're still living with your parents. Over 30 percent of young adults between the ages of twenty and thirty-four do (Vespa 2017).

The passengers. Despite the objective increases in actual support, many young adults across the country are also saying they are more stressed out, don't have enough social and emotional support, and feel lonely a lot of the time (American Psychological Association 2017). Emerging studies are finding that when parenting style blurs the line between support and overengagement, adult children report more anxiety, depression (LeMoyne and Buchanan 2011), and lower perceived self-worth (Nelson, Padilla-Walker, and Nielson 2015). Sometimes, parents' best intentions of support may impede opportunities for growth through failure.

The autopilot reactivity. These same studies found a link between parental overengagement and emerging adults' use of psychotropic medications and recreational use of pain meds. If our parents have always been there to fight our battles, reassure us, and clear the way of every obstacle, it will naturally be more difficult for us to skillfully tolerate on our own the uncertainties and obstacles that life offers. Too much support might wither your "figure it out" muscles and breed the above-noted UI.

Reassurance-seeking behaviors are those things we do to get others to help us reduce our anxiety, uncertainty, or insecurities. And yes, seeking reassurance from friends and parents is a helpful way to get another opinion. As an emotional habit pattern of reactivity, however, too much reassurance seeking has been found to contribute to a whole host of mental health challenges (Gillett and Mazza 2018). Researchers have linked it to the development of depression, obsessive-compulsive disorder symptoms, and generalized anxiety disorder. Overreliance on the reassurance habit only feeds the doubt and insecurity passengers as you never collect the life events you need to learn that you can handle them!

PAUSE. How much do you seek reassurance (from a person or Google) when you're anxious or uncertain? Could this emotional habit be keeping you stuck or obscuring opportunities for growth?

In sum, the increase in options, access, and parental support is likely to have put you in a precarious position. You may have higher expectations of what you think you should be accomplishing and how easy it "should" be. At the same time, there are the very real challenges of higher school debt and impossibly high costs of living. These are real sources of uncertainty and anxiety about your financial security, not just passengers! All of these factors together mean you have to be extra skillful to not get caught in the automatic pulls of the human ETA system. But it's worth considering how some of these road conditions might influence your worldview and ability to cope before we get to the exercises that will help you identify your unique passenger patterns.

Hijackings: How Your Past Messes with Your Present

The particularly difficult past experiences leave the toughest passengers of course—the old hurts, the bullies from middle school, mistakes our parents made, broken hearts, betrayals, and loss. These types of past experiences can add some pretty gruesome passengers. Like gangs of thugs, they distract and scare us; sometimes they slime the windshield so we can't see where we are going. So of course, when they show up, all we want to do is shut them the heck up! We start driving (doing and thinking) in ways that quiet them down and relieve our discomfort. We act in ways that distract, deny, or overcompensate—anything to keep the monsters out of awareness!

Even the simplest of situations can trigger passengers if you've had a difficult past experience that was remotely similar. For example, say you had a past experience where you were unceremoniously dumped via text message. Say this happened when you thought the relationship was going well, but there had been a brief delay since your last message was returned. In your next relationship, the next time there's a delay in response to a text, you might start getting anxious. The anxiety and worry might compel you to send repeated texts for reassurance, which might unintentionally overwhelm your new beau. This could lead him or her to withdraw, of course triggering your passengers even more. Ultimately, your reaction to the passengers (not what the present-moment situation called for) would push your guy or girl away. You can see how our passenger-driven reactions can really stir up the trouble in our lives!

But what if you had already done the work to recognize your passengers? What if you could more mindfully catch when this was happening and then use your skills to manage your anxiety effectively? When we've done the hard work of clearly identifying our passengers, we can *choose* to respond differently, rather than react automatically. When we become mindfully self-aware, we are empowered to break the repeated patterns in our life that keep us stuck and make us miserable.

PAUSE. Think about a recent event when you reacted more strongly than the situation called for. You will learn how to identify your own passengers and patterns in chapter 5, but for now, consider how this strong reaction might have been passenger related.

Who's On Board? Taking Role Call

The whole point here, and goal of this book, is to start looking behind the problems you see on the surface. What you'll be looking for, and I hope you are starting to wonder about, are your own passengers and patterns. There are usually some star players and then the bit actors that don't cause too much trouble. In order to get more skillful with them, you need to get to know them better. The practice is turning *inward*: moving toward your emotions, rather than smothering them, ignoring them, or pretending they're not there.

LET'S PRACTICE: Taking Emotional Roll Call

Below is a QR code link to a video practice to start the brave work of turning your attention inward. In this practice, you'll start to get a felt sense of *how* to connect with your emotions and to check in with your passengers, before they have to scream to get your attention.

If you tried the exercise, bravo! Being a seeker isn't easy. The purpose of this visualization practice is to really get in there and bring you in contact with those vulnerable, and potentially uncomfortable, internal feelings. Different people will have different experiences. Many experience this practice as comforting and an opportunity to honor what is difficult. Others find it more challenging. In either case, we'll be coming back to this practice as a key way to start building a better relationship with your passengers.

In this chapter you were introduced to a new way of thinking about and relating to your internal experiences. Was it challenging for you to pause and take this kind of internal inventory? This work can certainly be challenging at times, illuminating at others. Most important, I hope you're beginning to see how these experiences are part of what makes you human. The journey is just beginning. I encourage you to stick with it as you learn how to take your passengers with you.

CHAPTER 4

Learning to Love Your Passengers

This being human is a guest house. Every morning a new arrival.

A joy, a depression, a meanness, some momentary awareness comes as an unexpected visitor. Welcome and entertain them all! Even if they are a crowd of sorrows, who violently sweep your house empty of its furniture, still, treat each guest honorably. He may be clearing you out for some new delight.

The dark thought, the shame, the malice, meet them at the door laughing and invite them in. Be grateful for whatever comes because each has been sent as a guide from beyond.

> —Jelaluddin Rumi, "A Guest House,"
> translated by Coleman Barks

It wasn't until the end of a session with Nina one evening that a hint slipped out about a difficult passenger with which she was struggling. As a classic castle dweller, she made a huge effort to push down her uncertainty passenger and related feelings of doubt and anxiety. But this evening, something was going on just beneath the level of her awareness, as she told me all the reasons she was choosing not to attend an important work event that weekend.

It seemed out of character for her to choose not to go. Knowing her perfectionistic self-expectations, I continued to inquire. "Are all of those reasons as important as the office event?" I asked. My continued inquiry began to crack the shell of what was really bothering her. "No, they're not!" she said with some irritation in her voice. "I just don't feel comfortable going, that's all." Ah! A hint! The old "I don't feel comfortable" reason. I had an entry point! We explored the discomfort to find that Nina's perfectionism extended beyond just her work and social environment. She also had unrelentingly high standards for, and judgments about, her appearance.

Here too, her perfectionism habit was getting in the way of being effective toward reaching her goals. "I don't really care what they think. It's just that the party is at my boss's house. I don't have anything to wear. And I don't want to subject myself to their judgments." So that was it. Nina was assuming that others would have the same unrelentingly high standards and judgments as she did. While she may have been correct in this assumption, the assertion that she didn't care was clearly not true. She was judging herself through the eyes of others and, more problematically, judging herself for caring. Nina could see that avoiding the event, and the anxiety it caused her, was driven by her perfectionism. But awareness that a passenger is present is just the first step. She needed to get in there, let go of her judgments, and allow a space for uncertainty to be on board. This chapter is about the frustratingly counterintuitive process of attending to our passengers in a new way, a kinder way. This chapter is about learning to love your passengers.

The Judge-and-Jury Problem

We all know the judge-and-jury passengers of course. These guys are constantly keeping us abreast of our expectations of how things "should be," when our expectations are not being met, and telling us "It's *not* okay!" Naturally, sometimes we need to make a judgment call about things to be effective. Making discrepancy judgments would have been an adaptive trait for our ancestors to avoid threats and stay alive. The onboard-discrepancy analyst can still come in handy for making effective day-to-day decisions, like when that cute guy is flirting with you but you remember that you met his girlfriend just the other day, or when you find that cool new restaurant online but when you get there, you see a big letter D grade in the window. Sometimes it's a good idea to listen to our internal judge.

More often, the inner critic's opinions and comparisons wreak havoc on our mood and emotional well-being. The team of cross-armed, furrow-browed opinionators can hurl their perception-distorting, mood- and motivation-sabotaging input at just about anything! The judgment brigade really does its damage when it starts turning on the other passengers. The judge and jury shout, "Hey, WTF is sadness doing here? I'm supposed to be happy!" or more subtly telling us, "This is stupid; I shouldn't be getting so upset." Remember the secondary emotion problem? If you want to get yourself worked up into a spiral of out-of-control emotions, then judging, ridiculing, and shaming yourself for your vulnerable feelings is the recipe!

When judgments are aimed at our self, we're at greater risk of depression and social anxiety. When aimed at others, anger and irritability aren't far behind. Either way, when these guys are up and active, when judging becomes like a thinking habit, the result is that we just can't see the good stuff as well anymore. This thinking pattern is being practiced and strengthened. At the same time, our ability to attend to the abundance in our life may begin to feel unnatural and wither because we haven't been practicing that way of thinking.

PAUSE. In your journal, make two lists. First list all the things you want to change. Nothing is too small. Go for it—kvetch away! Once you have that off your chest, make a similar list of all the small and large things that are currently *not wrong* in your life. When you're finished, take note of how you feel.

It's often easier to notice the positive once we have also acknowledged the difficulties in our life. But oftentimes, we get stuck in judging the judging. Nina, like a lot of my clients, was getting stuck because she was judging herself for caring. "I shouldn't let this bother me. I'm so much more fortunate than other people," she would say. So she was denying her own difficulty with doubt and uncertainty. I asked Nina, "If we know logically that judging yourself makes things so much worse, I'm wondering, what's getting in the way of you letting go of the judging?" Her answer was illuminating. "I feel like if I don't judge myself, I'm letting myself get away with it." And there it was! It turned out that the belief that she was, in a way, being proactive to "keep herself in line" was some very old programming. To Nina, letting go of unhelpful judgments just didn't *feel right.* Judging was so familiar, like an old toxic friend. So letting go, or "practicing acceptance," her mind told her, was giving up. She was caught in the classic double bind between what feels familiar and what works.

PAUSE. Take a moment to complete the following sentences (borrowed from Follette and Pistorello 2007) to get a hint about some old, judgmental belief passengers on board your vehicle. According to my parents, the worst quality for someone to have is _____, and the best quality for someone to have is _____.

Taking Passengers with You

So, right about now you may be thinking, *But my passengers are making me miserable! How can I not judge them? Can't I just get rid of them?* Most of us start out hoping that someday, somehow, we will emerge from the issues that plague us as if they never happened. Poof! That thing that upsets you, that old insecurity or feeling you struggle with, will be gone! Well, let me ask you this question. Can you change your history?

PAUSE. Take a moment to sit with this question. Notice your whole-body reaction as you take this in.

Just as we can't delete your history, or change the past, I'm sorry to say, we cannot unprogram your programming. And you cannot unknow what you have been exposed to. Your passengers are coming with you on your journey into and through adulthood. Part of you already knows this. As much as you may try to not feel the old insecurities, the doubt, the fears, or sadness related to situations that have caused you stress in the past, they always show up again at some point—particularly when you're faced with new or uncertain terrain on the road of life.

Your life is additive. As you progress into and through adulthood, you will collect more, new, and different experiences, which will add to your roster of passengers. But the things you do to try to appease, control, or suppress the ones already on board will just add more programming, which gives more juice to the passengers! Emotional habits are like feeding an angry dog that sits outside your door. If you want him to stop showing up, feeding him is *not* the way to go. So, maybe there's a paradox when it comes to taking your passengers with you that can help you enjoy the ride a bit more. Can you see that there might be another way, a more effective way, to work with the difficult passengers you've collected?

PAUSE. Let's take a moment to honor the universal difficulty we humans have with the feelings of vulnerability our passengers cause us. Place both hands on your chest, one on top of the other. Notice any thoughts or feelings that come up for you around the idea of taking passengers with you. Say to yourself, "Here is my suffering. This is part of what makes me human." Notice how this kinder, nonjudgmental approach to discomfort makes you feel.

Leaning into Acceptance with Willingness

It's the judgmental struggle with our internal discomfort that gets us caught in the paradox and turns the basic pains of life into larger suffering. Letting go of the struggle and acknowledging and allowing discomfort to come along for the ride may be the most difficult part of becoming an emotional grown-up. Letting go of the struggle is practicing acceptance.

Acceptance is highly unintuitive because it's the opposite of what our mind and body are compelled to do when we feel stressed or distressed. That's why you don't naturally know how to do it, and it's highly unlikely that someone has taught you. If you've ever learned how to snow ski, you know that terrifying feeling of being told by the instructor to lean downhill to regain control! *What?* Our instinct tells us to lean back, uphill, away from the danger. But that's not the effective thing to do. If you've been windsurfing, you know that fighting the wind head-on simply won't work. The key is to work with nature's force by catching the wind in your sails.

These paradoxical laws of nature also apply to working with your emotions. But to have a real, felt sense of the difference between struggling versus practicing acceptance, it's important to get in there and practice with your own here-and-now experience.

LET'S PRACTICE: Leaning into Discomfort: Bring It On!

Below you will find a QR code link to another guided practice. I strongly encourage you to check it out. I don't want you to just take my word for it. I want you to *feel* the difference between struggling and accepting from your own experience.

Acceptance is *not* resignation or throwing in the towel in disgust that we can't have our way, feel the way we want to feel, or make the changes we'd like in the world. The practice of acceptance is *proactively* tapping into the laws of nature governing how our mind-body vehicle functions. The empowerment of finding a flow in and around the challenges life throws at us comes when we balance our aims at *feeling* better with getting *better* at feeling (Hayes et al. 2006). So a more useful term for acceptance is *willingness*; the skill is actively choosing to lean into the dance of internal experiences (the good, bad, and ugly) as they show up along the road of life. The practice involves opening up to the tides of our emotions, the cascade of physical sensations, and the pushes and pulls of thoughts and feelings. Being skillful with emotions means slowing down to honor the feeling and then letting go of the defenses and reactions that automatically jump on us. Acceptance is the lubricant for the cogs in our emotion regulation system. It's what prevents us from falling prey to the rigidity of our emotional habits that get us stuck in our suffering. It's the furthest thing from giving up.

One of my favorite studies showed the direct effects of acceptance and willingness versus trying to control internal discomfort (Eifert and

Heffner 2003). Researchers divided people into two groups and exposed them to carbon dioxide gas to induce anxiety symptoms. (You know, shortness of breath, heart palpitations, and sweating; yeah, good times!) In one group, the subjects were taught to control their anxiety symptoms with deep breathing exercises. The other group was taught how to practice nonjudgmental acceptance, similar to what you'll be learning here. The people who were taught to try to control anxiety experienced more fear and catastrophic thinking, which naturally led to more avoidance, than those in the acceptance group. The people in the acceptance group actually experienced the same physical effects of the gas, but they reported feeling less distress!

PAUSE. What thoughts and feelings come up for you when you consider this idea of allowing discomfort—leaning into it, rather than fighting it? Does it feel daunting? Or hopeful? Something else?

Acceptance on the inside begins with the acknowledgment of life on life's terms—the hand we were dealt (the vehicle we inhabit and the passengers we've collected)—and then sets the stage for playing that hand as skillfully as possible. So, this type of acceptance of reality is a place to begin building the change you want in your life. In fact, some of the most recent research is showing that our ability to practice acceptance in our daily lives is the *most* predictive indicator of our mental health and ability to effectively regulate our emotions (Kotsou, Leys, and Fossion 2018).

Taking Ownership of Your Passengers and Your Life

It's delicate territory asking people to accept and own their own stuff— to recognize that the type of vehicle they inhabit and the passengers they've picked up influence how they perceive and react to the world.

It's not easy to face the realization that only *you* can make the changes you want in your own life. It's so much more cozy and familiar to live in the stories we tell ourselves about why things are as they are. Even if we're miserable, it's familiar.

Christopher reached out to me wanting to learn skills. When he came to my office, the first thing he said to me was, "You have to understand that I'm an empath, so I feel everyone else's feelings. I need you to teach me skills to stop picking up on everyone else's stuff." Due to the communication function of emotions, we can "pick up" and resonate with other people's feelings. But as long as he was glued to this story— that the emotions with which he was struggling were caused by someone else—he was stuck. After all, it was his experience we had to work with.

Who's to Blame?

This idea of "taking ownership" of our mental health can have a taste of *blaming* to it, don't you think? Blame is like the active component of judgment. It means "to find fault" and is usually associated with the responsible party. But what if there is no one to blame? You might be thinking, *How can you say that I can't blame the person, situation, or experience that happened or is happening right now?*

Here's the problem with holding on to blame: If we get stuck in the story of blame, who becomes the victim? Who has the power when we blame someone or something outside ourselves? When we hold on to the blame story, it doesn't serve us. It's a bit like what's called the *corpus delicti* problem in legal texts. The law states, "If there is no dead body, there cannot have been a crime." Similarly, when we hold tightly to our own stories of injustice as proof that our emotional difficulties are valid, we hold ourselves as the symbolic "dead body."

When we cling to the blame story, that is, "I am the way I am because I have been wronged," the blamer becomes the victim. So, by extension (our mind tells us), "If I am *not* a victim, there was no crime."

Letting go of blame can *feel* like we are letting someone off the hook. But who's really on the hook here? Who are we keeping stuck as the symbolic dead body? In short, holding on to blame—holding someone or something outside ourselves on the hook—only serves to keep us on the hook with them. When Christopher realized this, he learned that he held some pretty strong judgments about people who couldn't manage their anxiety. In this way, his castle side felt more comfortable attributing his anxiety to someone else. On the other hand, he wasn't wrong that his more village side could pick up on the emotions of others. He was getting himself caught on the hook as long as he clung to the need to find someone to blame!

"But," you might say, "I have all these extra passengers because my parents..." (did whatever they did to get those passengers on your vehicle and thus lead to where you are). You might say: "The situation that I am in is unfair!" Your boss is a jerk, the establishment doesn't care, or the baby boomers ruined the economy. Yes, these injustices may also be facts. And, again, I'm not saying that injustices have not happened. The point is that your parents (or whoever) acted according to these same laws of nature based on their past experience and how they learned to cope. So, we might blame their parents and experiences. But then who do we blame for their parents' behavior? This blame game would go on forever!

Would You Rather Be "Right" or Be Effective?

You can certainly continue to hold on to the blame and the stories that go with it. Or you can begin to practice identifying and letting go of those stories and accept that the nature of *all* humans, the laws of the biopsychosocial theory, have led things to be just as they are. As the Buddhists say, "Everything is exactly as it should be." That is, everything is exactly as it should be according to the way mind-body vehicles operate in the context of certain road conditions and experiences. With this view, if there is something to blame, it is simply the laws of nature.

Now, this doesn't mean we have to like, approve, or desire these circumstances to be so; acceptance is *not* the same as approval. Acceptance is simply coming to terms with the world on the world's terms in order to begin coping effectively and striving toward the changes we can make. Until Christopher could take ownership of his emotions, with acceptance, he would be unable to use the therapeutic processes and skills he needed to work with them. For him, and for all of us, this means taking responsibility for our own predicaments. Perhaps an easier way to think of it is like this: You may not be responsible for what happened to you in the past, but you can be response-able to do something different now, today, in the present moment, and moving forward (Hayes, Strosahl, and Wilson 2003).

LET'S PRACTICE: Letting Go of Judgment

Bring to mind an incident in your life about which you might be holding on to blame or judgment. In your journal, express all your grievances about the injustice. Notice how you feel. Once you've finished, go back and underline the *facts* (the who, what, where, and when, but *not* the why). Next, circle any emotions related to these facts. Finally, rewrite the same events without judgment of how things should or shouldn't have been and without causal interpretations. Could the same facts be written into a different story? Read through both descriptions and notice how they feel different.

This story-change exercise (borrowed from Follette and Pistorello 2007) may help you see that the facts as they happen are something very different from how our mind puts pieces of the story together around them. Could you feel a slight difference between being entangled in the judgment story versus simply noting the facts and related emotions? What if, instead of investing so much energy blaming and judging the outside or fighting your passengers inside (who aren't going anywhere anyway), you began working on building a better relationship with your passengers? As in any good relationship, that means finding the balance between leaning in and engaging, and stepping back and getting space.

Reparenting Your Passengers

You can also think of carrying your passengers as driving around in a car full of little kids. Thinking about our emotions this way can help us start relating to them with less judgment and more compassion. Like a good parent, it's your responsibility to take them with you as you go about doing the things you need to get done and being the adult you want to be. But as soon as you start heading in the direction of something, *anything* you care about, the kids start getting cranky! Remember, when we care about something, emotions are going to show up.

Anxiety shouts, "Oh gosh, are you sure? What if?" Dread, his twin brother, chimes in, "It's gonna be bad!" And you know that Irritated will wake up and really start screaming, "Why do we have to do this? This totally blows; UNFAIR!" When the kids start getting rowdy, it can be very difficult to do the things you need to do as an emotional grown-up! So here's the question: How does an excellent parent respond to an uprising of kids in the back seats? I'll give you multiple choices to make it easier:

A. "Shut up back there, or I'll give you something to be cranky about! What's wrong with you [insert expletives]? You're an idiot for getting upset!"

B. Mute ignoring: puts fingers in the ears or turns up the radio to drown them out.

C. "Oh my gosh! Okay, okay!" Goes wherever they tell her to go.

D. Pulls the car over. Crawls into the back seat to reassure and soothe them until the kids are quiet.

E. Kindly and compassionately acknowledges the kids are upset while continuing to move toward the destination. ("Yeah, I know, guys. I know this trip is [label the emotion]. And this is something we need to do to.")

Can you see that E is the balanced and skillful response in most cases? If you noticed a pull toward one of the other answers, that is great information to have! If you chose A, B, C, or D, that should tell you something about how you are currently attending to your passengers (and maybe how your parents attended to you). Your response might also give you a hint about your emotional habit patterns. Do you tend to lean toward overindulgence (reacting to your moods and beliefs as facts) or an overly punitive engagement (berating yourself or ignoring internal cues)?

PAUSE. Take note in your journal of your answer choice. Where does that automatic belief about how to attend to your feeling states come from?

Answers A and B are what we call invalidating responses. Both show disregard for the needs of the children and aim to change or block the message being sent. Invalidation happens when our internal experiences are judged, dismissed, or outright ignored. We all know how crummy that can feel. Just think about the last time you were freaking out about something and someone told you, "Calm down!" or "It's not that bad!" It's particularly hurtful for sensitive peeps. Sometimes, even when someone is trying to be helpful by saying, "You're fine!" or "It's not that big of a deal," it can feel lousy because we don't feel understood.

On the other hand, overengaging our internal experience can also be problematic. Answers C and D may suggest an overattentiveness to passengers and what's happening inside the vehicle rather than the demands of life outside. Answer C suggests a tendency to get hijacked by the emotion-action tendency link. At the extreme, this may be the kind of impulsive reactions to emotions that can get us into trouble. More frequently, they're those day-to-day ways we wait until we *feel like it* or just capitulate because it's too uncomfortable to change course.

Answer D may sound like a really loving thing to do. But think about it for a second. What if you listened to those passengers every time dread showed up before an obligation? Or if sadness made you feel so heavy in your body that you just didn't want to get out of bed? Overengagement of our passengers might be just as detrimental to our mental health as underengagement. In fact, thinking habits, like ruminating and worry, are the core mind habits of depressive and anxiety disorders. When you spend your life waiting until you "feel like it," the passengers are making decisions about your life, rather than you.

Mastering Adulthood with Acceptance and Change

The central dilemma in becoming an emotional grown-up is choosing when to practice acceptance and when to push for change. Mastering adulthood requires learning to balance skillful attention between the passengers inside and the facts on the road outside the vehicle. The recipe for the balance between acceptance and change needed in your world, to get you toward your goals, will be unique to you. We're all in a continuous process of choosing between the needs, wants, and desires on the inside versus those on the outside. Most of the time, the compromises we're making are just beneath the level of our awareness. The next chapters will give you the road map you need for identifying when to push, when to pull back, when to allow, and when to buckle down. Validating the passengers while holding your commitments to what's important on the road is what it all boils down to. The sum of your success will be defined by your willingness to flexibly hold the balance between acceptance and change.

PAUSE. Before we move forward, this is an excellent time to go back and read the reasons you listed at the end of chapter 4 for doing this work. It's important to have those reasons top of mind before you start the exciting work of mindfully turning inward and solving the great mystery of you.

PART II

UNIQUE YOU: GETTING SELF-AWARE

noise

STI

Calm Happy

peace

CHAPTER 5

Tuning In to Your Autopilot Patterns

The essence of bravery is being without self-deception.

—Pema Chödrön, *The Places That Scare You*

A long time ago, when I was still studying and freaking out about what to do with my life, my ability to do it, and how long it would take me, a yogi friend said, "You know, Lara, sometimes you gotta slow down to speed up." I stared in confusion. "Uh, what?" To me, what he was saying was so foreign, it was like he was speaking Alien. Slowing down goes completely against what feels natural when I'm excited or eager about something.

My friend was trying to gently encourage me to be more mindful of how my own autopilot emotional habits showed up when I was faced with situations that triggered passengers. Of course, I had no idea back then what my autopilot was or *how* to slow down and be more mindful. I just stumbled into one autopilot collision after the next, not understanding why the same kinds of scenarios repeatedly played out in my life.

Mindfulness skills can't protect you from the normal mayhem of life, of course. But knowing your own passengers and autopilot emotional habits can certainly help you avoid repeating the same mistakes over and over again and promote the resilience you need to bounce back. In this chapter, I'm going to introduce you to mindfulness as a skill for stepping back and building the self-awareness you need with passengers. This is a big chapter because you'll be learning your primary tool for identifying where you get triggered and the habitual ways you react. So, let's get started! Let's take a look at how you can apply mindfulness skills to know yourself better and start building the foundation for the life you want.

Mindfulness: What and Why?

Maybe you've heard something about mindfulness meditation as a self-help tool. Mindfulness is the new trend and ancient practice that helps us to recognize the relationship among the events in our life so life doesn't feel so random and so we can start taking ownership of the parts where we have some influence. It's gotten a lot of attention in recent years. From therapy rooms to boardrooms, and in hospitals, schools, and even prisons, mindfulness and meditation training are now practically considered mainstream. Over the past few decades, research showing the incredible benefits of practicing mindfulness has fueled public demand.

In the early 1980s, visionary Jon Kabat-Zinn began a program called mindfulness-based stress reduction (MBSR), using mindfulness meditation to help patients with chronic pain. The philosophies and practices have been found effective for a wide variety of stress and mental health–related problems. He defines mindfulness as "the awareness that emerges through paying attention on purpose, in the present moment, and nonjudgmentally to the unfolding of experience moment by moment" (Kabat-Zinn 1996, 145). Whew, I know! What a mouthful, right? To get past such heady definitions, MBSR teaches mindfulness skills through meditation. But mindfulness isn't just meditation; it's also a cognitive skill (Bishop 2004). With mindfulness, we increase awareness of our mental processes so we're more likely to make a conscious response rather than defaulting to our autopilot emotional habits. Five distinct processes underlie being mindful (Baer et al. 2006); these include (1) observing the relationship between external and internal events, (2) nonreactivity to inner experience, (3) nonjudging of experience, (4) acting with awareness or nondistraction, and (5) describing or labeling with words. So mindfulness is basically a skill set that helps us slow down and disentangle ourselves from those less-than-helpful things we do and ways we think, which get in the way of the life we want.

A lot of people think mindfulness means sitting on a cushion, tuning out the stress, and being really mellow. But that's not what mindfulness is at all. The skill you'll be learning here is *tuning in*, not tuning out from the stress in your life. Observing your internal reactions to stress mindfully will help you tune in to *your thing*—whatever that is, in a new way, a kinder, more skillful, and effective way. Kabat-Zinn says it's akin to "tuning your instrument" (1990). When we practice our skills, through meditation or other ways, we are honing our internal balance and resilience to stress.

Mindfulness is also much more than just a term or idea. You can't pick it up just by reading about it or watching a three-minute YouTube video. Mindfulness is an experience you feel inside your body, a way of being, a felt sense, which you acquire through practice. I do my best here to use words to convey this. But just as I can tell you all day long how it feels to go swimming or ride a bike, you won't have a clue until you *feel* it. So, let's practice.

LET'S PRACTICE: Breath, Body, Sound Meditation

Scan the QR code for a video of a brief mindfulness check-in practice.

As you moved your mind through the steps in the video, could you *feel* a sense of slowing down, of dropping in, and of getting present from the observer place? With practice, you can build this felt sense of dropping into the present moment and stepping out of autopilot reactivity as you tackle the business of adulting. Stress and uncertainty become more manageable. Make sure to take a moment to journal about your experience with this short meditation.

Just Sitting There: Formal Practice

The sitting meditation that you just did is called a *formal practice*. Building a formal practice of your own is a sure way to supercharge the concepts we've been discussing and the skills you'll be learning. But if you didn't feel super relaxed or all "Zen," that definitely doesn't mean you did it "wrong." During sitting practice, it's very common for some people to experience a new awareness of discomfort because usually we're distracted by all kinds of other stuff. When you start actively turning attention to the here and now, some uneasiness might show up. Because you are literally just sitting there, anything that does show up (thoughts, feelings, sensations, emotions) is by definition on board the vehicle. And if it's on board the vehicle, no matter how it got there, it's your job to know about it so you can start working with it more skillfully. A big part of mindfulness meditation, and being skillful, is practicing getting comfortable with discomfort!

Demystifying You with Informal Practices

The fantastic thing about mindfulness is that it's a fundamentally customizable tool for self-discovery and working with and through discomfort. So, if you felt that just sitting still is *way* outside your comfort zone, you've got options! After all, the goal is not about getting stellar at sitting on a cushion. The goal is to start checking in with your internal experience in a nonjudgmental way so you can recognize when you're getting pulled into autopilot—and then choose a more skillful response. So it helps to have a tool for building this moment-to-moment awareness in your daily life.

Learning to Read the Dashboard

Imagine you're driving along and suddenly your car starts sputtering, pulling to the left, and generally not doing what you need it to do. Where's the first place you look when there's a problem? You check the gauges on the dashboard, of course, to see what's in need of attention! Mindfulness is like checking the dashboard of your mind-body vehicle.

I developed the dashboard practice as a mindfulness-in-daily-living tool. The dashboard form is your mind-body check-in tool to guide the process of checking in with your experience, rather than pushing it away. Its purpose is to guide you to attend to, and distinguish, the five components of experience (the facts, emotions, thoughts, bodily sensations, and action impulses), which are always happening at any given moment. Each and every moment, the components of the dashboard are feeding into your ETA regulator, which underlies your mood and

motivation. With practice, you'll start to recognize the relationship between your experiences inside the vehicle, versus the facts outside. Compartmentalizing each in this way will help you to identify the passengers on board your vehicle and your reactive emotional habit patterns.

LET'S PRACTICE: Dashboarding the Present Moment

On a page in your journal, list the five components of experience as shown in the sample dashboard below. Set the timer on your phone for three minutes. Sitting quietly with your pen hovering over the page, attend to the components of your present-moment experience. In real time, write a few words about the *content* within each *component* as it shows up. Make sure to write down something for each component. You can also download a copy of the dashboard form and a detailed instruction sheet at http://www.newharbinger.com/41931.

Table 5.1. *Dashboard*

Components	Content
Situation and Facts	*I'm lying here on my bed, reading this book.*
Thought(s)	*I'm not sure what to write. This is silly.*
Emotions(s)	*Doubt, annoyance*
Bodily Sensation(s)	*My elbow pushing on the bed, a little tension between my eyes.*
Action Impulse(s)	*Continue reading without doing the practice. But do it anyway!*

Were you able to enter observer mode and track the coming and going of your present-moment experience, as it showed up, in real time? You have just practiced the essence of mindfulness! Actively stepping back, observing, and nonjudgmentally describing the distinct components of experience as they show up is mindfulness. The *content* of each component is constantly in flux, but the components are always there, underlying your more global perceptions of them as being pleasant or unpleasant. When you practice observing and describing in this way, you are hacking into the ETA system to start interrupting the autopilot. As the saying goes, "Awareness is the first step!"

Did you notice that some parts of your experience were easier to identify? That tends to be the case. If there was one component you had more difficulty identifying, it's important to do your best to find something going on in that area because each component holds important information about your passengers and the skills you'll need. This practice will be the primary tool you'll be using throughout and beyond this book. Ultimately, this will also be your data-collection tool. From the dashboard experiences you collect, you will be finding your passengers and demystifying your emotional habit patterns, ultimately to get more skillful rather than reactive to the triggers in your life!

Identifying and Setting Targets

In behavioral therapy, we call the thing we are working on changing a *target behavior*. But that can be a bit confusing. After all, we're looking at your holistic system of interactions as an ecosystem of behavior; each component feeds into and from the whole. The goal is to get in there and see what components you can tinker with to get the change in outcome you're after.

PAUSE. Go back to the page in your journal where you wrote your goals for this book. Consider any additions you'd like to target. Go ahead, be bold!

Sometimes the change we want is obvious, sometimes less so. Many people pick up a book like this one wanting to reduce their mood or anxiety symptoms. If you got this book because certain emotions are making you miserable, then you want to figure out how the other components are feeding that. But if you're looking for motivation on your path, then you might be looking for emotions or thoughts that are making it tough for you to commit to your direction. Regardless of what it is you want to change, the goal of collecting dashboards is to uncover the other components that are feeding what's challenging you.

Collecting Your Data

In the days and weeks to come, you'll be going on a fact-finding mission. This is the beginning of the journey to solve the great mystery of you! You'll be uncovering what triggers you and what's getting in the way of making the changes you want to make. To start collecting your data, you can print several PDF copies of the dashboard form (at the URL noted above), or you can keep a record in your journal. All you have to do is plug your experiences into the form as close in time as possible to when you notice (a) you're having a heightened emotional reaction or got really stressed out, (b) you're avoiding or procrastinating doing something you need to do (including the practices in this book!), or (c) you did the target behavior you want to change.

As with any good assessment, the more information you collect, the more accurate a picture you'll get of your autopilot profile. You'll need to do *at least* eight to twelve dashboards to start to see a pattern. Keep collecting them as you proceed through the book. The process of dashboarding will build your ability to step back and untangle the emotions, thoughts, and action impulses that lead to under- or overregulation in your ETA system. As you practice mindfully parsing out your experience in this way, you will begin to see the relationship between events.

PAUSE. How many dashboards are you willing to complete in order to discover your patterns? Make a commitment to yourself to do what is needed to find your patterns.

Identifying Patterns: The Relationship Between Events

Let's take a look at how patterns can show up and some of the trickier spots in figuring them out. We want the insights from your self-assessment to be as accurate as possible. So, let's look at some common patterns and sticking points as they showed up for our castle girl Nina, our village girl Jessica, and Amy, who is somewhere in between a castle and village girl.

Nina: A Classic Castle Pattern

As a classic castle girl, Nina's autopilot habits of perfectionism and minimizing difficulty made it tough to get in there and find her patterns at first. In her early submissions, she had trouble identifying her thoughts, images, and assumptions as distinct from the here-and-now facts. She would frequently either leave the thought component blank or enter something like "It doesn't matter" or "I don't care"—classic castle-style minimization thoughts! But those weren't the thoughts related to the anxiety she was experiencing. She obviously did care or she wouldn't have been getting anxious!

Table 5.2. *Nina's Dashboard*

Components	Content
Situation and Facts	*Task assigned to me that I've never done before*
Thought(s)	*I don't know how. I'll fail. I can't ask for help!*
Emotions(s)	*Doubt, anxiety, irritation*
Bodily Sensation(s)	*Antsy, tightness, stiff*
Action Impulse(s)	*Figure it out, push harder, shut down*

It was only after she had completed several dashboards that she began to see her pattern more clearly. Whenever Nina was faced with something new or unpredictable, she naturally experienced some heightened tension. What Nina didn't notice at first was how her automatic-thinking attempts to minimize her anxiety were really masking other underlying assumptions. If you relate to Nina as a castle person, keep an eye out for getting stuck in *assumption land* when identifying your thoughts.

Notice how each piece of Nina's experience was feeding into the ETA system. She was equating *I don't know how* with the prediction *I'll fail.* These thoughts naturally cranked up her anxiety. Second, recall that in the past, Nina had experiences in which asking her parents for help led to feeling smothered. For her, there was also an underlying assumption that asking directly for help was not an option. Figuring it out herself had always been the only solution. She would get stuck because the more her anxiety increased, the more she would double down on her perfectionistic aims and the less flexible and open she would be to consider alternative solutions. At this point, she would just shut down. Asking for the help she needed didn't actually occur to her. The image below shows how her uncertainty passenger was at the center of her ETA reactivity. Her assumption thoughts led to more anxiety; shutting down led to less of the support she really needed.

Nina's ETA Regulator

PAUSE. Can you relate to Nina? Do perfectionistic expectations about your performance sometimes lead to even less productivity or block creative problem solving?

Thoughts vs. Facts

In your first dashboard practice above, were you able to parse out the difference between thoughts (images, ideas, predictions, assumptions, memories, the stories your mind offers) and facts? The important thing to remember about this difference is that you're not looking for whether a thought or memory that you have is actually *true* or not. You're just building your ability to see a thought as a thought rather than a fact. It can get tricky.

PAUSE. Choose an object around you and run your hand along it. In your journal describe your experience of the object.

Did you write something like "desk" or "book"? Or were you able to connect to the *direct experiences* of the texture, edges, firmness, and so forth? Often when I ask clients to run their hand along the sofa or table, they will say they feel "glass" or "material." But is that really what is felt in your experience when you touch something? How do you know?

You "know" because of all your past interactions with other similar things. You have *learned* the label for objects that look like a desk or book. So, "desk" or "book" is actually your *interpretation* (based on past experience) of the color your eyes perceive and the shape, edges, or texture you feel. Your interpretation may (or may not) be correct. The skill of separating thoughts from facts is not about being right or wrong. The skill being practiced here is the ability to see thoughts for what they are—something different from the facts—even if they are an accurate interpretation.

When completing your dashboard forms, facts should be anything you perceive with your *direct experience* in the present moment, or the who, what, when, and where (not the why) that everyone would agree upon. This may seem like a silly way to compartmentalize your experience. But separating your thoughts from the direct experience in this way opens up a space where alternative interpretations may be considered. This skill will be essential when evaluating more emotionally laden sticky thoughts about facts. When we mix up thoughts and facts, it's a slippery slope to react (emotionally and behaviorally) to our mind rather than the facts as they are.

Jessica: A Villager's Pattern

As a sensitive village girl, Jessica had some super creative ways of using words to describe her experience. One week, her loneliness and abandonment passengers were particularly up and active following a call with her mom when Mom wasn't able to stay on the phone. In the dashboard related to that situation, the relationship between how she felt in her body and her thoughts and beliefs became clear. As you can see in her dashboard below, the elaborate way she used language to express her physical sensations added significantly more to the facts.

Table 5.3. *Jessica's Dashboard*

Components	Content
Situation and Facts	*Called Mom for support. She couldn't talk.*
Thought(s)	*Heart is coming out of my chest. Tarantulas inside my skin. Nobody cares! Not fair!*
Emotions(s)	*Loneliness, anxiety, anger*
Bodily Sensation(s)	*Hot face, chest pounding, itching, agitation*
Action Impulse(s)	*Cry, keep Mom on the phone, yell, and make her understand*

The words we use to think about and describe our present-moment experience can have a significant impact on the other components of the ETA system. Notice how the facts of the situation were actually rather benign. It does happen that sometimes, when we are in need, the conflicting needs of the other person mean that person cannot be available for us. (Note to reader: If you notice that your parents have an uncanny ability to push your buttons, that is completely normal. After all, they installed them!) As a sensitive soul village person, feelings of disconnection were literally physically excruciating for dear Jessica.

It became pretty clear that situations where she could not connect with others were a real trigger for her. She linked this back to early experiences when she felt invisible to her parents unless she was in crisis. So she developed the unconscious assumption that the rule was "If I am in crisis, others should, and must, pay attention to me."

But notice something important in her dashboard. For Jessica, the physical discomfort of agitation and itching was heightened by both the way she described them (who wouldn't freak out about tarantulas) and the belief that others should help her get rid of her terrible discomfort. All of this passenger activity inside the vehicle would frequently lead to Jessica escalating beyond what was effective for maintaining her relationship goals in the long run.

Crying and holding her mom on the phone probably worked and was appropriate when she was younger. But now, when Mom (or anyone else) began setting limits with Jessica, her mind yelled, *Not fair!* This activated anger and resulted in exactly the behavior that pushed others away and made people less likely to want to spend time with her. Now the important thing to remember is that, like most of us, Jessica was completely unaware that she was doing this! For sensitive village peeps, it can feel like you have twenty antennae, picking up all the subtle invalidations and hurts, where other people have only one or two. This can often feel like others just don't understand you.

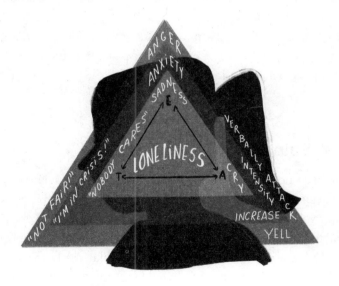

Jessica's ETA Regulator

PAUSE. Do you relate to Jessica as a sensitive village person? Is disconnection a trigger for you? Do you tend to use particularly descriptive language to heighten communication (to yourself or others) about your discomfort?

Thoughts vs. Bodily Sensations

Were you able to find words to label your bodily sensations in your dashboard practice? As we saw with Jessica, the blurring of the edges between physical sensations and interpretative thoughts can lead to lots of intense emotions. Actually, the essence of a panic attack is a misinterpretation (*OMG, I'm dying!*) of bodily sensations (chest pounding, shortness of breath), which feeds the emotion (fear), which exacerbates the physical sensations (heart racing), and so on.

PAUSE. Right now, take a moment to identify the specific, even subtle, physical sensations you are experiencing. We're always feeling something. (If you are not, maybe you should call 911!) Words to identify sensations might include "sharp" or "dull," or you might describe touch, temperature, tingling, tension, pressure, or pain. Also, be sure to locate the sensations in a particular area of the body.

Amy: A Vulnerable Castle Pattern

If you've been noticing that sometimes you can totally relate to Jessica and her deep need for connection, creativity, and vulnerability to loneliness, but you can also relate to Nina and her drive for success, perfectionism, and independence, then you just might be a vulnerable castle dweller! Vulnerable castle peeps appear just like castle folks on first glance, but their walls are more vulnerable to collapsing under pressure. For Amy, her apparent competence could get her the job interview or charm her way through a dinner party. But, beneath the façade was a super sensitive soul struggling to protect herself from deep fears of powerlessness and disrespect.

Table 5.4. *Amy's Dashboard*

Components	Content
Situation and Facts	*Six-month anniversary with Zack*
Thought(s)	*He's so awesome! What if he leaves? He's not that great. I could do better. Others will judge me!*
Emotions(s)	*Love, excited, doubt, irritated, anxious*
Bodily Sensation(s)	*Shortness of breath, forehead tension, chest pounding, shoulder tension*
Action Impulse(s)	*Overoffer, cling, nitpick, complain*

When triggered, Amy had particular difficulty differentiating her thoughts from her emotions. Those old familiar powerless passengers (from being bullied in middle school) made it very difficult to step back and defuse from the virtual reality her sticky thoughts created. If she *felt* powerless, it must be true, her mind told her. Her vulnerable feelings would send her mind hunting outside herself for a source of these feelings. Before she knew it, she was reacting in her body language and voice tone to her emotions and thoughts, rather than the facts of the situation.

Amy's difficulties stemmed from flip-flopping from a castle to a village pattern. This made romantic relationships particularly rocky because she did not yet possess the skill set for flexibly navigating the transition from wall up to wall down! Amy would become bewildered about arguments she was having with her boyfriend Zack. She was totally unable to figure out how a great night could blow up, with seemingly no provocation. In the image below, you can see how the content of her dashboard fed into her ETA system. The tug of affection would actually trigger her powerless passenger. Her worry thoughts would lead to clingy overoffering behaviors. But often, this would lead to feelings of resentment for all that she did for him. Other times, she would judge him and worry how others might judge her for being with him, which would lead to her picking at him with small criticisms. Then she would worry that she had pushed him away! All of this led to intense relationships that burned bright but fizzled fast.

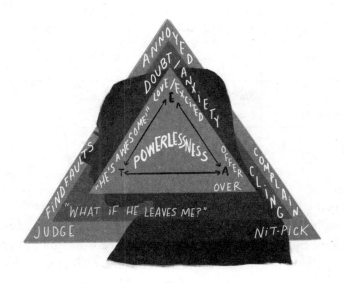

Amy's ETA Regulator

PAUSE. Have you ever noticed how difficult it is to recall details (thoughts) after a strong emotional reaction? Have you ever wondered after an argument, *How the heck did we get there?* Your dashboarding skills will help you solve mysteries like this.

Thoughts vs. Emotions

Remember, our emotions can blur how we perceive and recollect events. Similarly, thoughts can create a virtual reality to which we react emotionally. While the emotions we experience are actually a result of the holistic interactions in the system, for dashboarding purposes, you'll want to parse them out specifically. It's very common for us to confuse what we're thinking with what we're feeling. When we say, "I just feel like it will always be this way," or "It feels like...[anything]," those are thoughts.

Practice tip. Notice when you describe your thoughts and beliefs with the prefix "I feel like..." Practice stepping back from thoughts by saying, "I'm having the thought..." instead. This simple way of speaking about the content in your mind will help reduce some of the sticky-thought impact on your emotions.

Getting good at labeling your distinct emotions is an essential skill. Very cool new research has found that *affect labeling*, as psychologists call it, actually reduces reactivity in the brain and across all the other components of the ETA (Torre and Lieberman 2018). But words like "stressed," "hurt," and "bad" don't give us any information about the message of the emotion. So, it's important to use specific words, such as "sadness," "anger," "anxiety," "shame," "fear," "love," "joy," "happiness," and so forth. If you find you have trouble finding words for your emotions, there's a detailed table in chapter 10 that can help.

It's essential to be clear on the distinction between emotions and thoughts because the way to work skillfully with each will differ. Consider this: Think of a food you despise, one that really makes you gag. If I gave you a million dollars, could you just start loving that food as much as a food you crave? Could you actually experience it as pleasant and enjoyable? Of course not! You know from your own experience that we can't just decide to feel different about something when we already feel a particular way. Could you come up with thoughts and reasons to encourage yourself to take the action of eating the food and make yummy sounds for a million dollars? Yeah, probably. We have more influence over what we think and do. So, making the distinction between what you think about a fact and how you feel emotionally is going to be super important later for deciding which skill to apply to which piece of your internal experience.

Observing and Describing Action Impulses

The last place on the dashboard falls in the space just between an emotion and the action impulse in your ETA system. For village girl Jessica, it was the impulse to increase the intensity and seek reassurance when loneliness and anxiety showed up. For castle girl Nina, the impulse was to push harder when uncertain or anxious. And for our vulnerable castle girl Amy, she would flip-flop from overingratiating to overassertive actions. But in that space—just before the action takes place—is where your freedom to choose resides! This is a super important component because our action impulse is frequently aimed at calming down passengers but ineffective toward meeting our goals. It's here where you can gain the most control over your life.

Of course, before we wake up and tune in with mindfulness, many of the choices we make are outside our awareness, so they certainly don't feel like they are in our control. The cookies are there; we eat them. The drug is offered and taken. The thing we have always done to feel better is repeated. We are stimulus-response-stimulus-response *doings* rather than mindful, conscious human *beings*. The last component of awareness is noticing and recording what action you took or felt like taking in reaction to the others. Even if the action is "nothing," be as specific as you can. That is still the choice that was made, consciously or unconsciously.

PAUSE. Let's practice parsing out the difference between dashboard components. Read the following scenario. In your journal, parse the facts from the thoughts, from the emotion, and from the impulse.

Stan hasn't called me back! He's such an asshole!

I'm so pissed off I feel like breaking up with him!

Finding Your Unique Emotional Habit Patterns

During the coming weeks, as you continue to read this book, you will be looking for your own patterns in the information you collect. Just as you saw in the examples above, you're looking for commonly occurring *content* within each *component* and how it *functions* in relation to other component content on your forms. For example, is there an emotion that you are recording more than any other emotion? What types of thoughts, sensations, or impulses are linked to that emotion? Does one increase or decrease the other? Or is there a particular type of fact or situation that triggers you? What pattern shows up in these situations? If you really want to get in there and do the step-by-step analysis, you can download Steps for Identifying Your Patterns at http://www .newharbinger.com/41931.

PAUSE. Are you willing and committed to start collecting dashboards about your experience? Right now, grab your phone. Add a daily reminder or pick a time at the end of each day when you will maintain this commitment.

The dashboard exercise is a pivotal practice for taking ownership of your passengers and emotional habit patterns and for skillfully managing the challenges of your life. As you collect dashboard experiences in the coming days and weeks, the next chapter will help you get a better sense of what you want a life beyond adulting to look like.

CHAPTER 6

Setting Your GPS for True North

The good life is a process, not a state of being.
It is a direction, not a destination.

—Carl Rogers, *On Becoming a Person*

What direction do you want your life to be going in? Do you have some clear ideas about what you want your life to look like in the coming years? Maybe you know you want to find that thing that lights you up and makes a difference, but you just haven't found it yet. Setting a clear intention for the direction you want your life to take, rather than just bouncing along in reaction to what's thrown at you, can be astonishingly difficult!

On the continuum between holding your stuff together behind the castle walls and connecting and living authentically as a villager, there are three classic ways in which you might get caught in the proverbial quarter-life crisis. This chapter is about identifying your own *true north* and how to stay the course through the uncertainty that comes up along the way.

Your Own True North: Identifying Values

Every day and moment to moment, you're making decisions about which way to turn on the road of life. As you've come to see, oftentimes, these choices are outside your awareness because of past programming of uncomfortable passengers. As soon as you move toward something you care about, BAM! Those bad boys are up and out of their seats trying to get you off track. So how do you maintain your internal motivation when passengers are distracting you from what's truly important to you? You need a tool to help keep you motivated and focused with your eye on the prize of the success you're after. You need to identify your own true north on the GPS of your mind-body vehicle.

The internal compass of your *values* determines true north: your values are what *you* (not your parents, friends, or significant other) care deeply about and what you want to stand for in this lifetime. When you're lost and decisions need to be made, true north is there to guide you. Values are not the same as goals or moral directives. Unlike goals, they are not outcomes; the box is never checked; values are never finished. They are an overarching direction you want your life to take (for example, being healthy, independent, a caring partner). Goals (losing weight, getting a job, becoming a better listener) are simply the mile markers that can tell you if you are headed in the right direction.

Identifying them can be some of the most difficult work you do. Precisely because the instant you even start thinking about what you *really* want and care about, passengers are going to show up. But like the magnetic field that pulls a compass needle in the right direction, values also keep you on course. That pull of your values gets you through the difficulty and discomfort. Knowing what you hold near and dear makes the pain of passengers more worth it! Conversely, without a clear identification of what that is for you, the passengers have greater control over your vehicle. So, let's start homing in on your values by broadly identifying what life areas are most important to you right now.

LET'S PRACTICE: What's Important Now?

Review the life areas below. In your journal, rate their degree of importance, from 0 (being not at all important) to 100 (being extremely important) in your life currently.

- Career and development
- Friendships
- Leisure and fun
- Parenting
- Family of origin
- Community and political activities

- Romantic relationship
- Financial security
- Health, wellness, and self-care
- Education
- Spirituality
- Other:

This step will help get you aimed at the areas of your life that are most important for you to work on right now. At the same time, it's important for you to know that forward movement into and throughout adulthood is iterative. In other words, what you care deeply about—your values—may shift around at different times in your life. Right now, career or relationships might be most important to you. Later, perhaps parenting, health, or financial security will top the list. So, you may choose to return to this chapter as circumstances in your life dictate to explore your values anew.

PAUSE. Choose the three life areas you rated as most important. In your journal, rate how actively you've been working toward related goals. Lack of activity in an area, which you rated as highly important, suggests that this is a good area to start looking for passengers, and later using your skills.

What Do You Want to Stand For?

Within each life area, there is the kind of person you would like to be and become—an ongoing purpose for which you would like to stand. Identifying these values can get murky because our mind starts to offer up all sorts of distracting chatter. You may worry what others will think if you value something different. Or you may predict all the difficulties of pursuing your deepest desires. So instead, you stand motionless, paralyzed by the uncertainty of how to move forward. Values can help pull you out of the paralysis and motivate you to create a vibrant life you love. So, let's get clear on what you want to stand for and decide where to step first and what to prioritize.

PAUSE. Refer to the life area(s) you listed as most important and that have had the least activity. For each, complete the following sentences in your journal: "In this life area, it's important to me to be the kind of person who..." "I would like to demonstrate this value in my actions by..." As best you can, come up with about three to five keywords that really connect you to your value.

The Pause practice above gives you a concrete way to start getting at your values. If you're feeling stuck, consider people you admire in the area(s) you chose. Your role models may come from history, current events, or the movies. If you find yourself feeling blocked or second-guessing yourself, you might want to dashboard to see what thoughts or emotions are getting in the way right now. Typically, there are three common roadblocks to moving toward values, which may be similar for you where you're standing.

Traversing Uncertainty in the Quarter-Life Crisis

Recent surveys suggest that as many as 75 percent of twenty-five- to thirty-three-year-olds have experienced a quarter-life crisis (LinkedIn 2017). As you probably know, this is a time when uncertainty, feelings of insecurity, and doubt take hold about career, relationships, and finances. Some feelings of angst during this time have always been a normal part of entering adulthood. But in a world where social media is in your face, fostering comparisons and competition, and career shifting has literally doubled in the past year (as of the time of this writing), UI has become a big roadblock for many young adults. Standing in a place of the uncertainty of "not knowing," "knowing…but…!" and "caring too much" are three ways the uncertainty passenger may be hijacking you!

PAUSE. Is lack of certainty related to your ability, your life circumstances, or the likelihood of specific outcomes making it difficult for you to connect with what you would like your life to stand for, your values?

Standing in a Place of Not Knowing

Nina was feeling really stuck and uncertain about the direction she wanted her life to go in as her twenty-seventh birthday approached. She knew she was fortunate to be working at a big player in the entertainment industry. But about a year or so in, the shine started to wear off her idealized image. She spent long parts of her day working on admin stuff, which she hated. Worse still, on the few occasions she did get to interact with the senior execs, "They seemed like assholes. That's not who I want to be!" Soon, she was seriously thinking, *Why am I doing this? Is this really what I want my life to be about?*

Nina had a real quagmire here. Her job paid well compared with what most of her friends were making. She was really trying to "be positive" about it because she wanted to be smart about setting up her long-term financial security. But as the days, weeks, and months dragged on, each day she left the office thinking, *There goes another day of my life.* She felt more and more hollow, uninspired, and "blah." But she didn't know what she needed to make her happy. Yep! She was having a quarter-life crisis.

PAUSE. Is this where you are? Has the paralysis of not knowing for sure what you care about got you stuck?

Stepping into Uncertainty

Sometimes the quarter-life crisis sneaks up unexpectedly. Like Nina, maybe until now you've had a fairly easy time of getting things done, tackling responsibilities, and meeting the immediate demands of your life. When you're younger, life is kind of laid out for you: The demands of school, extracurricular activities, and social engagements are easily identifiable. You wake up at a certain time on school days, do your chores, and ask your parents for direction or when you need help. Even if it hasn't always been easy, when you're at home, or still in school, the choices are more clear-cut.

But now, standing at the edge of the vast unknown of your adult life ahead of you, it's you who are in the decision-making seat. Only you can dig down deep to find what kind of life will bring you fulfillment. Turning inward, toward the uncertainty, is likely to be uncomfortable at first. We humans generally do not enjoy this type of contemplative inquiry because we love certainty! We'll do just about anything to avoid uncertainty.

Bizarrely, studies have found that people will actually choose to receive an electrical shock rather than sit with uncertainty or contemplate their own thoughts (De Berker et al. 2016). This ironic attachment to certainty and avoidance of sitting with thoughts can have obvious consequences for identifying and setting your life path. Unfortunately, in order for you to get to that lovely place of knowing what you do care deeply about, you have to traverse that wide-open space of uncertainty. You have to build your ability to "sit in the not knowing" because from there, you enter the place of possibilities.

When you're at this juncture of not knowing, feeling uncertain, or simply not motivated, you need to connect across the great divide from not knowing to your values as your true north. When you're having trouble identifying the values to guide you—what you care deeply about—there's a space you can grab hold of to start getting some clues.

Connecting to Your Aha Moment

You know that moment when you meet someone that you instantly really like? Or when you find that one pair of shoes, handbag, or cool gadget that just jumps out at you? Your eyebrows go up. You feel yourself straighten up a bit. There is an energy in your body. That is an aha moment!

PAUSE. As best you can, bring to mind an aha moment in your life, where something in your life just clicked. It can be any little thing as described above or something more meaningful. It might be an area of study or interest, a place to live, a hobby, artistic expressions, or a person. In your journal, write about how it made you feel (emotionally and physically), why it inspired you (your thoughts and beliefs), and how it might have motivated you (your action impulses). These are the components of your internal experience (from the dashboard) that connect you to what it feels like when you have an aha moment.

When people talk about the things they value, you can see their eyes widen or well up. They speak more intensely, with more focus. The energy shifts when they're connected to what they care about. But if you've got a strong castle wall like Nina or you've suffered with depression for long periods of time, these feelings may be difficult to tap into. Emotional habits like minimization (I-don't-care-itis), blunting, or substance abuse might make reconnecting to authentic feelings of inspiration take a bit more time. So if you're drawing a blank, that's okay. Not every exercise works for everyone. There's always another way in! While joy and vitality tell you that you're moving toward true north, you can also get some direction from connecting to other emotions. Remember, your emotions carry the messages about what you care about.

LET'S PRACTICE: Connecting with Music

Pick two or three pieces of music that really touch you: one inspiring and one either sad or angry. Go find them, online or in your music collection. First, practice listening to and connecting with the piece you chose that brings you feelings of inspiration, joy, or vitality. Tap into the emotions that come up. If you are able to connect to the aha of joy, inspiration, or hope, journal about the related thoughts or images of a future you. Next, listen to the sad and angry music. For these pieces, explore in your journal what might be the loss or injustice you feel and what value this might represent for you. Is there something there that you need to pursue?

A sense of vitality comes when you progressively take actions consistent with your values in meaningful ways. But your uncomfortable emotions also carry messages about what is meaningful to you. If you chose a sad song, ask yourself this, What is the loss I associated with this song? If you can identify what that loss is for you, then that will tell you something important about what you *care* about, what you want more of in your life. If you chose to connect to a song that brought up anger, ask yourself, What is it that feels unfair to me? Anger suggests an injustice. If it pisses you off, then you must care about it, right? So what is the wrong that needs to be righted in some way? How might you work to right this type of wrong in your world?

Nina chose "Unwritten" by Natasha Bedingfield as her inspired song. It turned out to perfectly validate her uncertainty and encapsulate her deeper untapped value. The lyrics and tone helped to connect her to uncertainty as a place of inspiration. Her nostalgia for the '90s took her a little old-school with Meredith Brooks's "Bitch" as her angry song. This helped her tap into her feelings of injustice around having to maintain a job that really didn't represent who she wanted to be. She realized that a big part of her conflict was still trying to appease her parents' worries by showing that she had a stable job. These feelings helped her recognize that she really did want to have a space where she could take more risks, be messy, and be imperfect. With this new insight, she was able to identify the value of allowing herself to take a few more risks and show up more authentically at work and in her relationships.

Standing in a Place of "I Know, But…!"

The second part of the UI is the "I know, but…!" barrier. As noted, as soon as we get a hint of knowing what we care about, a bluster of thoughts and feelings related to what could go wrong tend to show up. Jessica was deeply connected to her value of creativity and her goal of being a writer. When she was struggling with the anxiety and sadness of her loneliness and abandonment passengers, creative writing had always been a means for her to feel grounded. For her, translating her thoughts and feelings into the eloquent expression of written words brought her a laserlike focus and lightness in her body she didn't experience anytime else. She had journal upon journal of beautiful writing.

But when it came to applying this value to schoolwork or starting the blog she wanted to write, she never seemed to get around to it. When she felt lonely and couldn't connect with her mom or her boyfriend, her passengers would give her a million reasons to procrastinate. Each time we explored what was getting in the way of her commitments, she would reply, "I know, but…"

No Buts

A simple entrée into the creative space of sitting with uncertainty is the "no buts" rule. Remember, the ways we speak and think can have a huge impact on how we feel. For a little word, "but" can create big road-blocks. The word "but" actually means "be out" in Latin. When we say "but," we are actually saying, "be out with the first part of what I said." As a result, we feel more connected to the second half of what we said or thought. As a result, this little word actually holds us in an all-or-none place that can trap us. For Jessica, "but" was usually followed by the many reasons her mind gave her for why she couldn't write at a particular time: "I can't. I'm too distracted. It doesn't *feel* right." And this is the energy she got glued in, rather than the more empowering connection to what she knew in her heart of hearts: she wanted to write!

PAUSE. In your journal, write down the "I know, but..." aspiration you have. For example, "I know I want to pursue a career in _____, but I worry that _____." Allow that thought to roll around in your mind and notice how it feels. Next, write the same sentence using "and" instead of "but." Repeat and connect to your aspiration in this way in your mind. Notice how it feels to think or say your aspiration in this way.

Were you able to get a sense of how changing the "but" to "and" opens up a space where both can be true at the same time? This simple "no buts" rule will help you to hold "both-ness" in your awareness. You can hold and carry this awareness that pursuing your true north is *both* what you want deeply *and* hard, scary, and uncertain. It will likely feel a bit awkward to replace "but" with "and" at first. Keep practicing. It is possible, essential even, to get skillful at holding *both* the image of where you want to go together with the passengers, difficult thoughts, and feelings that emerge when you do.

Practicing Holding the Both-ness

When Jessica was struggling to maintain her commitments to her writing, it took a while for her to figure out what exactly was getting in the way. After all, she really did value creativity and enjoyed writing, and she really did dream of making this her profession. We decided to do an exercise to really connect her with that dream and find any passengers that might be hijacking her.

If you can relate to having the big dream, a vision of what you want to be your life purpose, *and* you're feeling blocked in your forward movement, the next practice exercise is for you! Even if your true north is still a bit fuzzy, I encourage you to give the practice a try as it will help you to connect with the future possibilities you want. *And* it's also a concrete way to begin identifying, and working with, those subconscious passengers that get in the way of forward movement.

LET'S PRACTICE: Visualizing Success

Take some time to process what came up for you in this visualization. Did it energize you toward your goals? What were the rewarding properties you connected to that might help you stay motivated moving forward? If you found it challenging, identify the both-ness of what you want together with the difficulty. Make sure to journal what you visualized and your reaction to the practice.

When Jessica did this visualization, she had an unexpected reaction. She imagined her success, what she would be doing, and how it would feel. To her surprise, she became tearful as she imagined seeing her blog following grow and publishing with larger blogs like Elite Daily and Refinery29. When the practice was finished, I asked her to tell me more about her experience.

"Were you able to see the success you want?" I asked. "Yeah, I did," she replied, tearfully reaching for the tissue box. "It's just that I'm nowhere near there now. When I imagine all the work it will take to build a following and maintain it, it just feels overwhelming." As she explored further, she noted how heavy her body felt. Imagining her success did not actually connect her to the lightness and vitality of her true north. Instead she was pulled into how isolating and anxiety pro-voking it might be. This made her lose sight of the both-ness: the con-nection to her writing value of creative self-expression *and* the scary anticipation of her passengers. But the exercise helped her see exactly how she was getting hijacked, which set the stage for where her skills would be needed to hold on to the *both-ness.*

Did you have a similar, less-than-pleasant reaction to visualizing your success? If you did notice discomfort arise, good noticing! This exercise is what we call an *exposure* practice. Running the images of your goals through your mind like this *exposes* you to the passengers that are derailing you from your commitments. Visualizations like this are what sports psychologists do with athletes. The more you practice them and the more willing you are to come back to the visualization over and over again, the less hold the passengers will have over you. We'll discuss more about using exposure to practice being skillful with passengers later. For now, if you did experience difficult thoughts and feelings during this practice, I strongly encourage you to dashboard what you noticed come up. These are likely to be the kinds of thoughts and emotions to which you will later be applying your skills.

Standing in the Place of Caring Too Much

Caring too much is the third barrier that tends to come up when nego-tiating the space of uncertainty during a quarter-life crisis. Life fre-quently makes us choose between competing priorities among the things that are important to us. One of Amy's great qualities was that when she was excited about something, there was just about nothing that could stand in her way. Unfortunately, this led to a fair degree of impulsivity, which left one previously enticing project dangling as a new one caught her eye. Amy had several areas of interest. She was torn between her drive for success and financial freedom on one hand and her need for creative expression on the other. She also had strong values related to maintaining her work-life balance and spending time with her boyfriend. She rated all of these life areas as equally important.

Unfortunately, the conflicts among her goals related to the many things she cared about eventually led to her getting fired. One weekend, rationalizing that she was prioritizing her romantic relationship and creativity values, she got in the car with her boyfriend and headed out to Burning Man! Six months later, she was still unemployed, not wanting to make another "wrong" choice that might put her in a similar conflict.

PAUSE. Can you relate to Amy? Do you feel paralyzed by indecision either between life areas or different values within the same life area?

I asked Amy, "What if you could give equal time to all of your interests? What would it mean to you to be able to live all of your values, fully and authentically?" She paused, looking down poignantly, and then looked up with tears welling in her eyes. "It would mean I was living life right. That I had reached a place of…well, a special place, a place where, well, I was special. Untouchable. I wouldn't have to worry about the arbitrary rules others come up with because I would be living by my own rules."

Her answer was like a beam of light showing her passengers. "And so, if you don't or couldn't live in this 'right' way," I asked, "what would that mean to you if you put one or some things to the side for now?" She took a deep breath as if a thought surprised her. "I guess it does *feel* like I'm giving up my power!" And it suddenly became crystal clear to both of us. It was the same old powerless passenger hijacking her values path accompanied by its protégé, worry.

LET'S PRACTICE: Clarifying Values

In your journal, for each of your values, answer these questions (borrowed from Walser and Westrup 2007): What would it mean for you to live your life *currently* according to this value? What would it mean for you *not* to live this value at this point in your life? Even if they don't seem in conflict, your answers will further clarify why you want to stand for these things in your life and the limitations you might be faced with.

Practicing Acceptance of Limitations

Values themselves are rarely in conflict. It is possible to absolutely highly value many things at one time and pursue those values in varying degrees. Amy's value of work-life balance could support both her relationship and her financial security values. Maintaining this balance may help her be more engaged at work. And her love of music and creativity may support all of these values.

Sometimes however, our *goals* within our values will conflict, and so choices must be made about what to prioritize at any given point in our life. Chucking one value completely to the side, as Amy did, creates imbalance. Like the bars on a music equalizer, each slider may be raised or lowered to meet the frequency demands at a given time: the choices we make about which sounds (values) to emphasize and when to create the harmony we manifest. Raising them all at one time, however, will only create chaos and static. As you compose the symphony of your life, you must choose which tones and which instruments will take priority. Moment to moment and day to day, you live the music you create and want to dance to and the life you wish to build.

With every choice, there will be costs and benefits. If you turn left, you will feel the pangs of loss for what was on the right. If you turn right, you will feel the pangs of loss from the left. The following is a simple practice for working with life's limitations, which can help when you're faced with this uncomfortable place of caring too much.

PAUSE. Bring to mind any difficult thoughts and emotions that came up when you practiced the Visualizing Success exercise. Take a moment right now to put this book aside. Either close your eyes or just gaze out into the room where you are sitting. On your in-breath, compassionately say to yourself, "I'm inhaling with awareness." Honor the feelings of anxiety, frustration, or loss related to this goal. On the out-breath, say, "I'm exhaling with acceptance." You are accepting that life imposes some limitations in the service of our larger goals and values. Repeat this mantra to yourself several times: "I'm inhaling with awareness. I'm exhaling with acceptance."

This short practice can help you feel a sense of holding the middle between honoring the loss of what is desired *and* accepting that life comes with some limitations. This mantra may be helpful for all kinds of small and larger choice points: when you want to eat the whole pizza, *and* your value is to be healthy; when you want to watch another episode, *and* your value is being alert the next day for work. You are staying the course to true north and taking discomfort with you. You are holding awareness of both-ness in the face of uncertainty and making some difficult choices in prioritizing your goals. This chapter was about getting you connected with your big-picture source of caring, which makes the challenges of forging through uncertainty worth it! Where do we go from here? Read on, brave traveler! In the next chapter, you will learn how to apply this new awareness to your goals and commitments.

CHAPTER 7

Putting Your Vehicle in Gear: Making a Commitment

If you do not change direction, you may end up where you are heading.

—Lao Tzu, *Tao Te Ching*

When you want your life to go in a particular direction and autopilot isn't getting you there, it's time to take control of the vehicle! It's time to set some clear intentions and shift into manual—or mindful—overdrive. Have you been completing and collecting your dashboard forms to find what's no longer working in your life? As your patterns start to emerge, you're likely to see how certain thinking and feeling passengers are derailing you from living your true-north values. In this chapter, we're going to identify some commitments you can make from a place of mindful intention, rather than autopilot.

Where Values and Willingness Meet: Commitment

It's no mystery that making and keeping commitments is hard work. As we saw in the last chapter, knowing what you care deeply about can be inspiring and daunting. Holding conscious awareness of what you deeply want *and* not yet moving toward a value can compel you right back into your autopilot patterns. So, you have to get crystal clear about setting the baby-step commitments that will get your started. To maintain those commitments for the long haul, you will need to link the warm, soft space of self-compassionate acceptance with the necessary harder spaces of self-discipline and commitment with willingness.

Willingness to override your autopilot means taking the discomfort with you, moment to moment, as you pursue the direction you want your life to take. It's starting from where you are, rather than where you would like to be or think you should be. It's a *choice* you can make. So the road map to mastering adulthood looks like this: keep your eye (and mind) on true north—while practicing willingness and skillfulness with the discomfort that comes up—as you commit to actions that move you in the right direction.

PAUSE. As you shift gears toward making a change, what thoughts and feelings start to show up for you? Can you simply observe these experiences as they show up *and* be willing to forge ahead in the service of your values?

Willingness vs. Willfulness

Choosing *not* to be willing is called *willfulness*. Willfulness is fighting reality—battling the facts, your passengers, and the dashboard components of your current experience—in an unskillful way. It's like when you have a case of the "screw its." Part of you, the observer part, knows that you're resisting doing what the situation calls for to be effective toward your goals, but passengers and emotional habits win the battle for your attention.

Willingness isn't the same as *wanting* or "feeling like" doing something; it's simply taking the steps needed to be effective. Both Jessica and Amy had a tough time with this distinction. Despite knowing she deeply valued creative expression and wanted to be a writer, Jessica firmly believed she could write only when she felt like it. Certainly, particularly for an act of creativity, it is more ideal to do things when we feel like it. It's even likely that writing will be more productive when one feels like it. But what if the feeling doesn't come when the behavior is needed?

Amy got really stuck on the idea of willingness versus wanting, which caused another argument with her boyfriend. She wanted him to go with her to couples therapy to help build their communication skills. He said that he was willing to go, no problem. Still, she wasn't convinced. "It feels like if he *really wanted* to go, he would take more initiative, like remind me and put it on our calendar." As we explored deeper, she revealed the belief that "People don't do things or make changes unless they want to." So I asked her, "Is it possible that he is willing to go to couples therapy for the long-term value of your relationship even if he doesn't feel like it?" We discovered that to accept this, her mind told her she was "forcing him to go," and somehow it was her passengers that were the cause of them going. This interaction helped us crack the shell of her own willfulness around being in this place of vulnerability with her boyfriend. (The powerless passenger strikes again!) Ultimately, in the service of her values for the relationship she came to a place of willingness to accept her own feelings of powerlessness.

Without values awareness, we're just white-knuckling it! Willingness is *accepting* the short-term discomfort in the service of our longer-term values-driven goals. So, we need clarity about our values to know why willingness is worth it. Of course, we all get willful sometimes. The key is to get good at noticing when willfulness is getting in the way of moving toward true north. Choosing to allow discomfort, in the service of your values, is simply making a choice among the limited options of more of the same (not moving toward your values) or something different and unknown.

PAUSE. Bring to mind a recent event in which you were being willful—a choice-point moment when you knew you were acting against your values and did it anyway. In your journal, dashboard the separate components of what was happening. Which part of reality in that moment were you *not* accepting?

It's also worth recalling here how your ETA system gets rigid in either overregulator or underregulator mode. Of course, it's much easier to take an action when you *feel* like it. *And* it is also true that when you change your actions, it is highly likely to change how you feel. Have you ever pushed yourself to go to the gym when you didn't feel like it or to go out with friends even if you were tired? Then once you got there, you were really glad you did! Yeah, it's like that.

Willingness Is All-or-None; Commitments Are Negotiable

You might feel yourself in that wobbly place of wanting change, but only being "kinda sorta willing" to have the discomfort of uncertainty. Yeah, I get it. A lot of people get stuck because they're on the fence about willingness. But here's the deal: Willingness is like jumping. You may choose to take big jumps, like from a desk to the floor. Or you can choose to take smaller jumps, like from a chair to the floor or even from one step to the next. Regardless of how large the leap to which you commit, there will always be a space of uncertainty, where you're in the air and uncertainty has to come with you. Trying to sort of, kind of be willing is just more of the same willful struggle with discomfort.

When Nina discovered her true-north value of wanting more authentic relationships in her life, it became painfully clear that she needed to make some life changes. Since, until now, her life was completely organized around her perfectionism, her choices had always been made with a goal of being "the best." When she tapped into this important missing piece, her mind immediately raced toward planning gigantic leaps.

"How can I do this?" she begged. "I'm not going to just quit my job and move to a kibbutz!" Nina's mind raced off into the new undefined territory in the same way she had always thought about things, imagining herself living the *most* authentic life. So of course, she started to feel overwhelmed and anxious. Nina was applying the same perfectionistic extremes to this new value. The good news is, whether you've been speeding along in one direction, like Nina, or stagnant with little direction, like Jessica, changing direction is incremental. So, while willingness is all-or-none, commitment begins with baby steps.

Two Types of Commitment

Getting out of the emotional habits that keep you stuck or derail your goals takes two types of commitment: taking actions in the true-north direction and practicing your skills. Each will support the other in moving your life forward in the direction you want. These two types of commitment will be iterative. In other words, when you take action toward true north, you will need your skills. Practicing your skills, on a regular basis, will help you maintain your commitment toward your goals. The larger the commitment, the more skillful you'll need to be because more passengers will try to get in your way!

Heading North: Taking Action on Your Path

Committed action is what we do with our hands, feet, and voice that moves us, in any increment, toward that adult we want to be. Commitment is not an idea or belief about what you stand for; commitment is an action! No commitment is "too small" or "pointless." I can't tell you how often I see the minimization-thought passenger show up for people as soon as it comes time to move forward on commitments. Thoughts like, *I can do it later. I'll remember; it will be okay. It's not that important.* Notice when this happens because it will! We get so focused on the bigger goals we judge to be more significant that we get stuck at step one. Let's take that first step now and identify some moves you can take toward true north.

PAUSE. Choose the value you identified in the last chapter that has the least amount of activity in your life. Identify three small and *doable* actions you can take *this coming week* that reflect that value. Write them down in a prominent place in your journal.

Did you take this first jump into willingness and write down your commitments? At every tiny step along the way, take note of what gets in the way of taking the action. If you didn't write them down, what "reasons" did your mind give you? Our minds are natural reason-giving machines. And those reasons may be true. We get into trouble when our mind starts telling us that reasons are causes, which is *not* true.

PAUSE. If you had to choose between watching Fox News or CNN, which would you choose? Why? I'm sure you have lots and lots of good reasons. Now, even with all those good reasons, could you still turn the TV or web browser to the other channel and rest your eyes on the screen? How about if I gave you 10,000 bucks? Reasons may lead to choices; they are not *causes*.

Making the first commitment move was really a challenge for Nina. After all, by definition, to be authentic meant she would have to lower her castle wall sometimes so others could see a bit of those vulnerable places she was so used to covering up. Nina really wanted to move in this direction. She knew allowing herself to show a bit more vulnerability would mean having better relationships, increasing her sense of community and support, and helping her decide if her job was the right place for her. And yet, she squirmed in her seat just considering doing things in a less-than-perfect way, intentionally! We considered the very smallest of actions to get her moving.

To identify these small jumps into commitment, Nina made a list of *all* the situations she could think of that would cause her anxiety related to her uncertainty passenger and being "imperfect." By identifying the most obvious ones first, it was easier to find the baby steps to get moving. She put the possible scenarios in order from scariest to least scary and rated how much anxiety (on a scale of 0 to 100) she imagined she would experience for each. She committed to the three lowest items on the hierarchy first.

PAUSE. Make your list of any and all actions you can take that would move you toward the true north of your values. Then organize them from easiest to most difficult, rating how much distress you imagine each may cause you. Choose the bottom three for your commitments this week. Keep this handy, you'll refer back to these activities as opportunities to practice later.

Beyond just moving you toward being the grown-up you want to be, these kinds of commitments serve two functions. Each time you engage in the committed action, you are (1) practicing with passengers and learning you can handle it and (2) investigating whether the dreaded outcome actually happens. So now that you have your three commitments written down, create your reminders. Before reading on, add your commitments to your calendar or set an alarm at a particular time each day to remind you to do the actions you identified.

Committing to Practice: Building Your Skills

In the upcoming chapters, the practices are broken down according to the components of the ETA system. Each component of the ETA system requires a different type of care. So the skills in these chapters correspond to the most effective to practice for each piece of your experience. Here, you will learn the skills to begin listening to and *validating* your emotions, stepping back from and *checking* your thoughts, and *changing* your actions to support your progress toward the adult you want to be.

Naturally, all of the processes are interacting at somewhat the same time. The dashboards you have been collecting are intended to help you build self-awareness of the relationship among these events inside your mind-body vehicle. The practices will teach you the essential skills of *how* to work with those internal experiences, as they come up, most effectively. Just as you wouldn't want to mix up the needs of your car (such as putting brake fluid in the steering fluid reservoir or oil in the gas tank), it's important to apply certain skills to certain pieces of your experience.

Some of the practices are shorter skills, which you'll be able to apply as you're going about your day-to-day life. Others are longer meditations and visualization practices. Many of the skills will have either QR codes for the videos or URLs to the audio files. These experiential practices will help you build a foundation of healthy, flexible emotion regulation. Ultimately, your goal will be to collect skills from each chapter to apply to each component of your ETA system as these experiences show up for you. As you work through the next three chapters, take note of the skills you find most helpful in your journal or on the Goals and Commitments worksheet. In chapter 12, you'll return to those skills to create your personalized Mindful-Mastery Practice Plan.

The iterative processes of commitment to values and commitment to skills is how you start transitioning out of your autopilot emotional habits, which keep your ETA system rigid, and into the life you want. As you shift into gear toward your values, some discomfort is likely to come up. As it does, you will be applying your skills to *validate* your emotions, *check* your thoughts, and *change* your actions in the direction you want to go.

Setting the GPS: Making Commitments That Stick

Whether you relate more to Nina and her full-steam-ahead autopilot or are more like Amy or Jessica and feeling a little willfulness and having trouble getting moving, there are some simple strategies that can help you maintain your commitments. As you proceed, use the following tools to help you stay committed. To help you stay organized, download the Goals and Commitments worksheet at htt p://www.newharbinger .com/41931. Let's go through these strategies briefly before getting started with the skills!

Set Goals, Not Outcomes

Goals are not outcomes. This may sound obvious, but many people imagine outcomes rather than goals when picturing the success they want. For example, if you'd like to find a new job related to your values, as above, you would identify all the possible actions *you can take* to move you in that direction. You might commit to finding three online job sites, working on your résumé, and finding and interviewing people who know about that profession.

Set Levels of Commitment

You want to set yourself up for success, so it's important to avoid getting into a pass-fail situation. To do this, set your practice goals and commitments in levels: optimal, acceptable, and passing. Set an *optimal* level as the most or best you could possibly do for that commitment. For example, if you want to start being more social, you could set an optimal commitment as going out with friends three times per week, an *acceptable* level as two times per week, and a *passing* level as one time per week. Similarly, I recommend that each week you set your own three levels of skills practice. For example, you might choose one or two skills each week and then set your levels of commitment to practice (for example, *optimally* could be four days per week, *acceptably* three days, and *passing* two days).

Make Practice a Priority

This is the hard part! Building your skills for flexibly moving in and out of your emotions is like going to the gym for your mental health. One thing you can plan on is that it will be challenging for you to get around to it. You might think about it as your regularly scheduled therapy appointment or meeting with a trainer. Find a time and a place each week when you can commit to regular practice and schedule it into your calendar.

Link New Behavior to Old Behavior

Another handy way to help you stay on course is to link the new behavior to an old one. For example, if you want to remember to complete your dashboard form every day, then you can make a deal with yourself that you will do it every day after you brush your teeth or when you get into bed. This strategy can also be linked to the next one.

Reward Yourself

Want to encourage a behavior (in yourself or someone else)? Reward it! For example, you can say, "If I complete X level of commitment, then I will treat myself to Y." Or you can be super disciplined and say, "If I don't complete X behavior, I will not get to have my usual Y." This can be extra motivating!

Team Up

Having someone to support you and cheerlead your progress is really helpful. Team up with a trusted friend who has similar goals and values. It's a fact that making public commitments is more likely to lead to maintaining them, so share your goals with someone you trust!

Remember Your Goals and Values

Whenever you feel your commitment getting wobbly (and it will), read through the values and goals you wrote down. You might put them somewhere in a prominent place, such as the notes app on your phone, so you can refer to them daily during this process. There will be days when you are on course and days where you divert a bit. The key is to stay close to the main road toward what you want, rather than getting distracted by what you don't want (by your passengers).

PAUSE. Before heading into the next section of the book, decide on and write down your commitment times, levels, and goals for practice in your journal. Set your calendar reminders or ask your phone's personal assistant to remind you. Once you've done this, write yourself a note about why this commitment is important to you. What will it mean for you to be more skillful?

Now that you've gotten an idea of the direction you want your life to take and set some initial steps to begin the journey, it's time to put your vehicle in gear and take action! It cannot be said often enough: change is hard! So be kind to yourself as you move forward on the commitments you've set. If you're feeling some discomfort, worry, or concern, that's awesome! You are right where you should be. As you push ahead, always remember this: growth comes in fits and starts; it is not linear. The skills you'll be learning will teach you *how* to get comfortable with discomfort.

PART III

SKILLFUL YOU: GETTING SKILLED UP FOR MASTERING ADULTHOOD

CHAPTER 8

Making Nice with Emotions: Validation Skills

Joy: *Isn't this fun?*

Anger: *Can I say a curse word now?*

Sadness: *Crying helps me slow down and obsess over the weight of life's problems.*

Disgust: *Well, I just saved our lives. Yeah, you're welcome.*

Fear: *Maybe it was a bear?*

—From the movie *Inside Out*

The animated movie *Inside Out* does an amazing job showing the complexities of the internal struggle we humans have with our difficult emotions. In the film, eleven-year-old Riley carries within her the five primary emotions, which play out as characters in the movie: Joy, Sadness, Fear, Disgust, and Anger. At the outset, Joy is running the show. Since Joy doesn't see the purpose of Sadness, she and the other emotions actively work to keep Sadness from touching anything in Riley's life. This has made Riley a happy-go-lucky girl, that is, until she's faced with her first major life change.

When her family moves from the Midwest to San Francisco, Riley doesn't know *how* to connect with and *validate* the sadness of the loss of having left her childhood home behind. Without the insight sadness can provide, Riley goes through a journey of struggles and mishaps. Ultimately Joy discovers Sadness's purpose: to connect and create empathy in those who are close to us. The movie ends (spoiler alert) with the whole gang of emotions accepting Sadness and her wisdom. Riley is able to adapt and begin creating new memories, as all the emotions work together to create a more harmonious internal life.

While the character in *Inside Out* was only eleven, this idea of accepting emotions is a new one for people of all ages. The science of the function of our emotions is new, so most of us don't have a good working knowledge of how to care for them in a skillful way. With all the challenges of mastering adulthood in the millennial age comes the benefit of knowing now what we didn't know before. Your emotions, all of them, serve an essential function in building an authentic, connected, and values-driven life. This chapter will help you build the skills you need for your emotional self-care: *validation* with self-compassion and willingness.

Preparing for Practice

On your journey through the book thus far, you've been learning, and hopefully experiencing from your dashboards and Pause practices, how struggling with your internal experience just adds extra suffering over the long run. You've learned how the emotional habits we use to avoid, control, and dismiss the messages of our emotions send us, like Riley, off track from the kind of adult we want to be. So you've been moving toward a space where you can begin relating differently to your emotions: less harshly, more openly. Skillfulness here begins by actively practicing getting better at *feeling*, to feel *better* for the long run.

There are two theories for why intentionally inviting in difficult emotions works to get you out of the ETA spiral and build your skillfulness. One is aimed at reducing discomfort; the other strives for acceptance and willingness to feel discomfort. Both are anchored in the traditional model of cognitive behavioral therapy (CBT) and have substantial research to back them up.

Traditional CBT-based skills aim to reduce anxiety and other uncomfortable emotions by achieving *habituation* or *extinction*. Habituation happens when your physiological and emotional reactions lessen following repeated exposures to the situations that trigger them. Extinction of a fear or anxiety response just means learning that you can handle it (that nothing bad happens to you from the exposure). You can probably think of lots of things in your life that once made you nervous but are now just things you do. For example, when you first learn to drive, you're anxious at first. But you just keep doing it until one day you realize it doesn't make you nervous anymore. The long-standing view is that repeated exposures, where discomfort is allowed to peak and decline *within* the period of exposure, leads to an overall reduction in anxiety (Moscovitch 2009).

More recently, the practices of mindfulness and acceptance, which you've been learning in this book, have been integrated into CBT. These *third-wave*, mindfulness-based CBT therapies emphasize *shifting our relationship* (less judgment, more acceptance, and kindness) to our internal experience. The aim here is to reduce the secondary reactivity, which is what causes the problems. Interestingly, more recent evidence suggests that it is not how much the emotion decreases during exposure but your *willingness* to allow the exposure that predicts longer-term improvements (Craske 2013). In other words, what really counts is your willingness to try!

In this chapter, we're going to dive into a series of practices, some of which were introduced in prior chapters, which will teach you *how* to care for your emotions with more willingness. Some will be shorter practices to use in your daily life; others will be more in-depth exercises to build your emotional flexibility and resilience over time. When you find a practice particularly helpful, make a note of it in your journal or on the Goals and Commitments form you downloaded from the New Harbinger website. You'll be circling back to them at the end of the book for your Mindful-Mastery Practice Plan.

Working with Your Here-and-Now Experience

To really know in your bones how to respond when your emotions get triggered in real life, you'll have to practice with real here-and-now emotions. Knowing something intellectually is much different than knowing it from inside your skin. So, a great way to learn how to be skillful before the next emotional trigger is to actively choose to invite in the emotions with which you need to practice. In experimental research that explores how emotions can affect or be affected by the other dashboard components, psychologists use techniques called *emotion induction*. Emotion induction simply means actively bringing up an emotional experience rather than just waiting to catch it as it pops up in real life. You can use these methods to get the most out of the skills in this chapter. The following is a list of simple ways you can bring emotions to the surface so that you can practice on your own terms with your actual experience.

- Listening to music and watching movies that evoke the emotion(s) with which you struggle

- Visualizing and journaling about distressing events

- Role-playing a common difficult scenario with a trusted friend

- Taking action toward your true-north values

PAUSE. Refer to your dashboard forms to see what specific emotions you identified most often. Compile a playlist of several songs and movies that are likely to bring up these same emotions so that you have them handy to use in this chapter.

As you go through the skills, begin with low-intensity emotions at first. For example, use music or bring to mind something that is only mildly upsetting to get the hang of how the practice works. Once you've gotten familiar with how a practice goes, increase the intensity each time. If you've been diagnosed with a mood or anxiety disorder (particularly due to traumatic life events), ask your therapist to help you move through the deeper exposures. Just as you wouldn't start bench-pressing super heavy weights without practice or a coach, slowly adjust the intensity to build your resilience over time. This building-up process will increase your emotional flexibility, which will help you navigate the triggers and stay committed on your journey to mastering adulthood.

Beginning in the Body

Do you ignore your body? Innumerable tiny signals are constantly sending messages and early warning signs about the effects of stress on our vehicle. For most of us, they're way outside our awareness. Instead, we tend to live in the heady problem-solving space of ruminating, worrying, and judging, which only gives more fuel to our emotions. For most of us, the related bodily sensations go way off the radar, until our emotions are screaming for our attention!

But our bodies are where emotions live—they are *embodied*. In the space between an emotion and the impulse to take action are physical changes in the body, which can alert us to get ahead of the emotion. The chest tightening, heaviness, and shortness of breath send bidirectional signals to the brain. Because of the back-and-forth influence between the body and our emotions, it's important to get good at mindfully tuning in to our physical sensations. When we get more in touch with our bodily sensations as a proxy for our emotions, we gain an excellent entry point for being skillful.

Connecting to Emotions in the Body

When you're getting stressed out and emotions are brewing, the first step is to start zeroing in with mindful awareness on the signs from your body. In the table below, you'll find some common bodily sensations and their related emotions. If you were having trouble labeling your bodily sensations on your dashboards, this table may be helpful. You may not feel all the sensations, but the idea is to start gently shifting attention into your body and scanning for early reactions. As I always say, "Minds time travel; bodies do not!" So, moving your attention in this way will help anchor you in the present moment, which will help you be more skillful in caring for your emotions. Listening to the signals of your body is the first essential step to anchor you during periods of stress.

Table 8.1. *Emotions and Typical Bodily Sensations*

Emotions	Bodily Sensations
Fear, anxiety, nervousness, surprise, excitement	Shoulder tension, chest pounding, shortness of breath, sweating, dizziness, eyes and mouth open
Anger, irritation, annoyance, frustration, disgust	Furrowed brow, corners of mouth down, upper lip tightened, chest pounding, squinting eyes
Sadness, despair, sorrow, grief, dejection, woe	Heaviness, lethargy, fatigue, teary eyes, head down
Happiness, joy, delight, pleasure, enjoyment, bliss, elation	Lightness, relaxation, warmth, widening of the eyes

LET'S PRACTICE: Body Scan

The Body Scan meditation is an excellent way to begin practicing checking in and connecting with your body to integrate your holistic system. In this audio practice, located at http://www.newharbinger.com/41931, you'll learn to move your attention, in a systematic way, to each body part. Barring any history of severe trauma, most people find this meditation highly pleasant and relaxing (Finucane and Mercer 2006). Most important, you'll gain a sense of agency from your own experience: what you do with your mind and your body has a powerful influence on how you feel. Attending and listening to your body, in a nonreactive way, creates a safe space in which you can anchor in the observer place. This practice has been related specifically to improvements in psychological well-being, including decreases in anxiety, physiological reactivity, and interpersonal sensitivity (Camrody and Baer 2008).

Anchoring in the Storm with Willingness

Willingness, the active choice of allowing discomfort, is the most powerful and essential skill for caring for your emotions. It also tends to be the most difficult precisely because it asks you to counter your hardwired human autopilot. This skill is so unintuitive; people almost always become frustrated with it. I can't tell you how often I hear, "How can I be willing to have my _____ (anxiety, depression, craving, or whatever) when it's making me so miserable?" It's highly likely that your mind will not want to be willing at first. However, we can get around the willfulness of our mind by beginning with willingness practice in the *body*. You can use the control you do have (over your body) to reduce the unhelpful secondary reactivity to emotions until your mind gets on board. I call this walking through the *willingness window* because this practice is a concrete action you can take to step into willingness.

LET'S PRACTICE: Willingness Hands

This acceptance skill (borrowed from dialectical behavior therapy, or DBT) is a simple body position you can take to actively practice gently allowing and letting go of reactivity to emotions. The Willingness Hands pose is a natural and neutral expression in the body. Because of those bidirectional messages between the body and mind, this pose sends a clear message to your mind that you are open to your experience, as it is. Evolutionarily speaking, you simply wouldn't take this action with your body if there were an actual threat (which is what your emotions are telling you). Remember, the aim is not to eliminate the discomfort. Instead, you are practicing letting go of the struggle and the secondary reactivity, which set you up for an ETA spiral. The subtlety of this skill makes it an excellent choice when you're faced with difficult situations in your day-to-day life. The steps are outlined below and in the video tutorial.

1. Use one of your emotion-induction techniques to bring to mind something with which you've been struggling.

2. Notice all the emotions, the types of thoughts, and where you feel your body tighten, become heavy, or get jittery. Take a mental snapshot.

3. Once you have connected to the discomfort, place both feet flat on the floor, while sitting upright, with your head and neck in alignment.

4. Extend both of your hands out, palms up, and slightly away from your body,

5. Allow your shoulders to drop away from your ears.

6. Extend your belly. Move your mind to intentionally *feel* your bodily sensations. Allow your experience to be just as it is. Take a mental snapshot.

Leaning In and Listening to Emotions

Remember, our emotions serve an essential communication function. So caring for them in a skillful way means getting close enough to listen and honor those messages. Anchoring in your body will help you slow down and stay present long enough to do this. As you move forward, it's the job of the caring grown-up part of you to attend and listen to the more childlike emotional parts in a new way, a more validating and compassionate way.

Validation: Your Emotional Elixir

Validating your emotions means taking a moment to honor the particular mind-body experience that is currently happening. Mindful validation might be a bit different from how we typically use the term validation. Here, we don't mean cheerleading or approving. Validation has no judgment of "good," "bad," or "should." When we validate, we're simply acknowledging that the experience is present. Much like in a parking garage when you get a ticket "validated" to show that you were in the building, here you are simply saying, "Emotions are in the house." In so doing, you're letting go of the *habit* of pushing them away. Validation is like the lubricant for the cogs in the wheels of the ETA system. It sets the stage for building the flexibility needed to take the bumps with more ease.

Developing a Validation Statement

One of the first skills I teach clients for working with difficult emotions is to have a prepared validation statement. This simple skill will help you generate more effective self-talk the next time you get triggered and emotions start to come up.

Step 1: Label the emotion. Remember, simply labeling your emotion can interrupt an ETA spiral (Torre and Lieberman 2018). Numerous studies have shown that labeling emotions (in yourself or someone else) activates the part of the brain known for logic and reasoning (the prefrontal cortex), which reduces activation in the emotion center (the amygdala). But more specifically, it has been shown that labeling emotions can improve the effectiveness of exposure exercises, similar to those you're learning here (Niles et al. 2015). So make sure to practice finding specific words to tag your emotions whenever possible. See the table in chapter 10, Emotions and Their Action Tendencies, if you need some help with this.

Step 2: Validate the BAH. The next step is to figure out why your emotion makes sense. Remember, all emotions make sense given the way your vehicle and historical passengers are interacting with the facts of the situation.

A handy acronym (if not terribly creative) for remembering possible causes of your emotions is BAH. Instead of "bah humbugging" or judging your emotion, validate the BAH. Ask yourself: Is there something *biological* happening for me today, making my vehicle more vulnerable? Would *anyone* feel this way in a similar situation? Is there something *historical* happening (Is this passenger related)? The table below outlines possible biological causes of vulnerability in your mind-body vehicle, which might be contributing to day-to-day shifts in your mood.

Table 8.2. *Biological Vulnerability Factors*

Sleep	Inconsistent or less-than-adequate sleep increases vulnerability.
Diet and nutrition	Processed foods and refined sugars increase inflammation and microbial imbalance in the gut, which can cause brain fog and other symptoms.
Lack of exercise	Numerous studies have shown that inactivity can make us more vulnerable to physiological stress reactivity.
Physical illness	Inflammation related to illness or infection can make us more moody. Continuous use of antibiotic or steroidal medications can also disrupt gut processing and nutrient absorption.
Mood-altering substances	Drugs and alcohol may reduce short-term stress but make us more vulnerable to rebound effects.
Hormonal cycles	Normal cycles of change, including monthly menstruation, pregnancy, and other developmental changes, impact mood.

LET'S PRACTICE: Your Validation Statement

Refer to one of your dashboard forms where you were triggered; you may also want to write down the following sentences in your journal. Practice validating your internal reaction by saying: "In situations where _____ happens, it makes sense that I would experience the emotion(s) of _____ (label or name the emotion) because (choose one or more of the following):

1. _____ (name the biological vulnerability factor) happened or is happening.

2. Anyone would feel this way in a similar situation.

3. Having experienced _____ (historical factors), my passengers (label them if you can) are stirring."

This sentence structure may seem a bit clunky at first. You can tweak it to sound more authentic to your ear. The goal is to begin relating to your experience in a way that is more validating, which will help reduce the secondary reactivity. Practice this new way of self-talk as an alternative to your habitual way of reacting when you notice you've been triggered or are just struggling with your day-to-day responsibilities.

Self-Compassion

Self-compassion actively promotes a sense of kindness toward oneself and connectedness to others in our humanity. Practices similar to the one below have been repeatedly linked to better mental health outcomes and life satisfaction (Neff and Germer 2017).

Self-compassion is practiced by offering yourself three qualities of attention: warmth, soothing voice tone, and touch. The aim is to step out of the self-critic mode and shift into mindful awareness and acceptance of your universal humanity. This skill connects you to both your own pain and the awareness that we all experience suffering sometimes. You are not alone! Self-compassion is an excellent practice for when you're caught in self-judgment, have the "why me?'s," or are feeling lonely or isolated.

LET'S PRACTICE: Steps for Self-Compassion

For this practice, choose a touch position you prefer. Try each of the following to see which resonates with you:

- Lay both hands, one over the other, on your chest.

- Place each hand across your chest on the outside of the opposite arm, as if you are giving yourself a hug.

- Place your hands gently on your cheeks.

- Place one fist on your chest and gently lay the other hand on top of it.

Next:

1. Assume the self-compassion posture you chose.

2. Use an emotion-induction technique to bring to mind a difficult situation with which you've been struggling.

3. In a warm and soothing voice tone, slowly say to yourself, "This is a moment of suffering. I see you there (label the emotion or passenger present). This is really hard right now. I honor that this suffering is part of being human. I am not alone in these feelings. May I be kind with myself."

Take note of how this practice made you feel. Self-compassion can feel a bit "woo-woo" at first. So go ahead and adjust the wording so it sounds more natural to your ear. The important thing is to find the *felt sense* of genuine self-caring and connectedness.

LET'S PRACTICE: Taking Emotional Roll Call

This visualization, introduced in chapter 3, guides you to check in with your passengers from time to time so you can maintain a better relationship with them. The guided imagery helps you actively practice nonjudgment, willingness, and self-compassion by giving otherwise shapeless experiences a physical form.

As before, you'll be asked to actively practice visualizing child versions of yourself on board your vehicle. This time, you will be asked to practice with an emotion or passenger you have identified in your dashboard forms. By physicalizing your emotions this way, it becomes a bit more manageable to practice acceptance of these parts of yourself.

PAUSE. How is your willingness as you dig deeper into these practices? Remember, you can do these at your own pace. While willingness is all-or-none, commitments are negotiable. If you've been skipping the experiential practices, try setting some levels of commitment (optimal, acceptable, and passing) to help you take some incremental steps forward.

Taking Willingness to the Next Level

Up to this point, you've been slowly wading into your emotions: getting to a place where you're ready to increase your experience working with more difficult emotions. In this section, you'll be building up your exposure to difficult emotions. The following practices will help you build your long-term emotional flexibility and resilience. So, are you ready to take it to the next level and start exposing yourself to those passengers and show them who's running the show?

Practicing with Exposure

These visualization exercises are intended to actively bring up and move you into your difficult emotions at a higher level of intensity. Remember, the whole point of practicing with exposure is to teach you that, as uncomfortable as they are, you can handle your emotions and related bodily sensations! It just takes some practice. Ideally, you will do each practice for five to ten minutes, or longer. It's essential to stay with the emotion for at least a minute or two, *past its peak intensity*. If you bail out of the exercise before the decrease, the relief you feel can reinforce the avoidance habit, so stick with it!

LET'S PRACTICE: Bring It On!

With practice, this visualization from chapter 4 will build your skill for entering the paradox of emotion regulation and psychological flexibility. You will be guided to invite in thoughts about something that bothers you so that you can practice being skillful in the presence of the augmented reality of your mind. Here, you will practice comparing what it feels like to get tangled up in struggling, judging, and trying to push away your discomfort versus being skillfully willing.

This time, refer to your dashboards to work with a situation that triggered more intense emotions. During the practice, you will be guided to shift between struggling and willingness.

LET'S PRACTICE: Visualizing Success, Overcoming Obstacles

If you've been having trouble connecting and committing to the direction you want your life to take, this practice from chapter 6 will be helpful. Moving your mind forward in time may either motivate you toward your goals or unearth any unconscious emotional blind spots (assumptions, bodily reactions, and related emotions) that may be blocking your progress. The practice brings you in contact with these experiences so you're practicing your willingness skill. Another added benefit is that what you find may be informative about other (thought and action) skills that you may use to stay on track with your commitments. In this practice you'll visualize yourself successfully accomplishing a valued outcome from one of the life areas you noted as very important.

PAUSE. How was your willingness with the last two practices? These were designed to help you hold the balance between acceptance and change. Now, we're moving into the deep end of exposure. Are you willing?

Making an Exposure Script

Traditional CBT exposure exercises such as the following can help you overcome your anxiety related to social situations, public speaking, or any tasks you need to complete to move you toward your true-north goals. For this one, go back to the hierarchy of stressful situations on the commitment list you made in the last chapter. Choose a situation that you imagine would cause you distress of at least a 40 or higher on a scale of 100. To be effective, pick something that is distressing enough to bring the emotions up, but not so distressing that you won't stick with the practice. Again, if you're working with a therapist, ask her or him to help you with this.

LET'S PRACTICE: Exposure to Uncertainty

In your journal, write a detailed script that describes your chosen situation. Describe the worst-case scenario as if you were writing a movie script. Who's there, what's happening, and what are you thinking? Also include the emotions and bodily sensations you imagine would happen. Be as creative as you can to write a first-person account of what you would be experiencing. Write your description in the *present tense* so it reads similar to this short example:

> I'm walking into my boss's office. She is sitting behind her desk, absorbed in what she is doing. I am about to ask her for a raise, and my heart is pounding like crazy. I'm worried that I'll piss her off and that she will think I am a joke for asking. I'm starting to sweat...

Record your script with your cell phone and make sure your recording lasts *at least* five minutes. Remember, the goal is to *feel* the emotions. To be most effective, hold your attention on the imagined scene. Notice any impulses to distract yourself or reduce your full engagement in the imagery. Anything you do in your mind to reduce the full impact will defeat the purpose of the practice.

Next, schedule a quiet time and place where you can sit or lie down and listen to and visualize your recording. Be with your emotions as they come up. Don't try to change them in any way. Allow the emotions to peak. Get them as strong as you can with the image fully engaged in your mind. When you reach the peak point, rate your emotions on a scale of 0 to 100, and stay with it!

Remember, the very last thing you want to do is jump ship when the distress gets high because this just reinforces the avoidance emotional habit, and you don't get an *extinction* response from learning that you can handle it. As you get to the end of the recording, continue to rate your distress in your mind. If your distress is still high, try the Willingness Hands practice to anchor in your body and the present moment and to help you bring your levels back to the acceptable range. Repeat this practice every day or so until you start to notice that it's becoming like a rerun movie that no longer has the same hold on you. Once you get to this point, repeat these steps with the next situation on your list. Keep going until you've mastered the scariest one! When you do, you are officially a willingness champion!

PAUSE. How's your willingness going? Have you been building up your ability to allow in and sit with discomfort? If not, return to your Goals and Commitments worksheet to remind yourself why this work is important to you.

Generating Good Vibes

After all this hard work inviting you (over and over again) to turn toward the difficult, practice willingness, and stay present to discomfort, you've earned some good vibes! After all, psychological flexibility—moving in and out of your emotions—isn't just about the difficult ones. It's also about strengthening your connections to the pleasant ones! These may not be getting as much attention if you've been struggling with the uncomfortable ones for a while. Since we become what we practice, let's practice generating some good vibes.

Practicing Loving-Kindness

Loving-kindness is a traditional Eastern meditation that is intended to cultivate attitudes of kindness and positive regard toward yourself and others. A recent study found that this type of practice has significant influences on both day-to-day and immediate positive emotions, such as happiness, pride, and self-esteem (Zeng et al. 2015). So, this is one you'll want to add to your list!

LET'S PRACTICE: Loving-Kindness Meditation

The mind is hardwired to seek out problems. Like all the psychological processes you've been learning about, this too served humans well in our evolutionary quest for survival. But as we move toward something more than just surviving, toward thriving and building a life we love, we need to override this instinct. This practice, available at http://www .newharbinger.com/41931, will help you build a nice strong connection to the abundance that's in your life, and likely open up a space for more in the future. In this audio practice, you will be guided to actively offer phrases of kindness and well wishes to yourself, to those who are very easy for you to love, and to those in your wider social circle. Ultimately you will be invited to send these same intentions to humanity at large and, if you are willing, even to those with whom you struggle.

PAUSE. This has been a challenging chapter! Take a moment to congratulate yourself for getting to this point. And then ask yourself, What small commitment might I make to practice these skills moving forward? Write your emotion validation skills commitment in your journal.

In this chapter, you learned some essential practices for caring for your emotions more skillfully in your daily life, as well as for building your emotional endurance for the long run. The *key* takeaway is that skillfulness with emotions means actively practicing kindness toward yourself when they come up. Here, you have learned step one: *Validate your emotions.* In the upcoming chapters, you will be learning the key steps for how to be skillful with your thoughts and actions.

CHAPTER 9

Keeping a Wise Eye on Thoughts: Check Skills

Nash: *Can you see him?*

Student: *Yeah.*

Nash: *Okay. I am always suspicious of new people. Now that I know you're real, who are you, and what can I do for you?*

—From the movie A *Beautiful Mind*

The movie A *Beautiful Mind* exemplifies one man's healing journey through and beyond the struggle with his mind. From the beginning of the movie, the main character, mathematician John Nash, is seen inter-acting with other characters which the audience assumes, as he does, are real people. As the movie proceeds, we slowly discover that the roommate, little girl, and CIA agent characters are all Nash's extra-sticky thoughts—they are hallucinations. Eventually, Nash develops this awareness too. He recognizes that there is a difference between what is fact and what his mind is telling him.

As is often the case, the first insight is the most painful. His strong beliefs and ideas were not true, and that hurts. At first, he fights with them. "You're not real! You're not real!" he screams as he struggles to push them away. This does nothing to appease them and even instigates them further, leaving him looking like the local madman on the Princeton campus.

Eventually, Nash lets go of his struggle. He stops trying to push the characters away. Instead, he makes the difficult decision to stop *reacting* to his old familiar friends and start *responding* more effectively. Unlike the movies however, practicing nonreactivity to passenger-related thoughts is far from intuitive and takes quite a bit of practice to master. Skillfulness begins with the humility that we are *all* prone to the tangles of our own mind. This gives us the self-compassion we need to let go of the struggle inside—to honor the passengers we carry—as we take them with us on our journey of mastering adulthood.

The end of the movie gives us a hint of what this looks like. Nash is shown still seeing his hallucinations. Because passengers never go away, sometimes they still try to get his attention. When they do, he doesn't yell at them or hide his eyes to prevent seeing them. Nor does he ruminate, judge, or worry about how they got there. Instead, we see Nash acknowledge the images his mind gives him with a subtle nod (validates them) and then turn his attention back to the present moment. He turns to his wife (what's important) while allowing the characters (passengers) to be there.

Where skillfulness with emotions requires leaning in and getting closer so you can *validate* them, working effectively with thoughts asks you to step back, observe, and keep your thoughts *in check*. In this chapter, you'll learn the skills to actively practice this type of decentering and disentangling thoughts from facts. There are three goals when working skillfully with thoughts:

1. Step back and observe the virtual reality narrative in your head.

2. Redirect your attention nonjudgmentally to the present moment.

3. Check your thoughts for accuracy to minimize reactivity to biased interpretations.

Awareness Is the First Step: Noticing Mind Habits

It's not easy to see thoughts for what they are: a mind activity. As a mind behavior, they too can fall into hidden habits just beneath the level of awareness. A good way to start thinking about mental habits is from the intersection of the present moment. Let's review four core mind habits. Like all habits, sometimes they're helpful, and sometimes they can backfire! Which ones do you tend to fall into?

Future Tripping

Most of us know this one. The mind is like an eager child, bouncing up and down on the back seat of your vehicle shouting, "What's next? What's next?", desperate to solve or predict problems before they're actually happening. This habit can be rewarding because it can lead to initiating new projects and sometimes preventing negative outcomes. Until it's not!

Worry about the future can also function as a kind of emotional habit. It gives the illusion of control over negative outcomes but keeps you stuck in anxiety. When the mind tends toward future tripping too often, "What's next?" can quickly morph into "Look out! Be careful!" It can feel like you need to engage the worry. The resulting increase in anxiety can lead to catastrophization, exaggeration of future problems, and eventually, burnout. It can also lead to propensity for hypomania, anxiety, and panic symptoms.

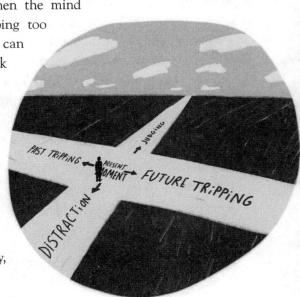

Past Tripping

Like a claw from another time that can jump up and grab you, this habit is related to thoughts of regret and loss: *If only...*, *Why me?* As you might imagine, or know from your own experience, this is the mind habit most often associated with past traumas and depression. Small reminders and triggers can easily activate old mind scripts, which activate the same old feelings and emotions. The mind repeatedly travels back in time as if it can solve the problem from long ago (which of course it can't). As a problem-solving machine, the mind searches for that just-right feeling of *why* this negative event happened.

The rewarding properties of chewing on old hurts are less obvious, but it's a bit like biting down on an aching tooth. The strong pain in some ways feels better than the dull ache. Revisiting an old hurt can also be self-validating to honor the sadness (Linehan 1993a). But as a mind habit, this way of thinking is almost guaranteed to hold you in a depressed mood. The ruminating mind just churns and churns over the negative thoughts and memories, spinning your ETA system into the downward spiral.

Judging

Judging the present moment, as you've learned, is the opposite of acceptance. It's an easy one to fall into when the present moment isn't as you would prefer it to be. This mind habit can be super tempting because it gives a small boost to how you feel about yourself compared to the target of your judgments. Judging is related to a sense of riotous indignation. "Not fair!" the mind shouts. But the almighty "shoulding" can be toxic. At its most malevolent, the judging mind may take pleasure in the failure of others, *schadenfreude*, which becomes a tasty morsel to distract you from your own stuff. Your opinions of how things should be hold you stuck in irritability, anger, envy, and hostility (or passive aggressiveness). If practiced over time, you no longer see your opinions as just that: opinions and not facts. This leads to grumpiness because the world is not accommodating your view of how things "should be."

Spacing Out and Distracting

In our tech-saturated world, spacing out and distracting are more and more common. There are so many awesome ways technology allows us to avoid thinking about our pain! This mind habit is an extra-slippery one and hard to catch in action. The temptation to space out gets addicting, not necessarily because it adds good feelings, but because checking out gives *relief* from whatever's bugging you. The path to a comfy space-out takes place so automatically that your mind just drifts off as soon as you're faced with something uncomfortable.

This autopilot mode can appear like an attention deficit, a lack of interest and motivation, or even narcissism. But it may also be associated with past trauma. In traumatic situations, this strategy can be helpful to minimize the suffering. But when it becomes a default mode, it can lead to obvious problems when you need to attend to the tasks of adulting! Difficulties in interpersonal relations often emerge because others take it personally when your mind wanders off at crucial moments. When life becomes uncomfortable or uninteresting, or you feel helpless to solve a current difficult problem, numbing out is a common reaction. Obviously, this habit impairs your ability to focus, attend to the demands of the environment, and maintain focus on tasks that require some tolerance of distress.

PAUSE. Where does your mind tend to hang out most? As you continue reading, set a mindful intention to catch any mind wandering. Anchor your attention in physical sensations, like your butt in the chair or feet on the floor, to practice staying present.

When Thoughts Go Bananas

A time-traveling mind can definitely pull you into an augmented reality, which distorts the present moment, diverting you from being effective as the adult you want to be. It really doesn't matter if your internal dialogue shows up in more severe forms (such as auditory hallucinations, obsessions, or racing thoughts) or more common worries, ruminations, or ADHD moments. The research strongly suggests that fighting your thoughts (suppressing them) only fuels them (Najmi and Wegner 2008).

PAUSE. Try it yourself. Right now, I am going to ask you to *not* think about something. Whatever you do, it's essential to not think about it. Ready? *Do not* think about a banana... What happened?

Yep, most people find that they immediately think about bananas when told not to. Of course, sometimes people get creative and say they intentionally distracted themselves with something else. Yet the bananas still dictated where your mind went because you had to actively bring something different to mind—not in the service of your goals and values, but to keep the bananas away (pun intended). Can you see that, if you make it essential that you *don't* think about something, the passenger is still running the show? What happens when you come across other things that remind you of bananas? Soon you won't be able to think or do anything related to bananas. You'll be playing a game of Whack-a-Mole with your thoughts until there's no room to think about anything else!

Reconnecting to the Observer

The core skill for working effectively with your thoughts lies somewhere between pushing them away and getting entangled in them. Psychologists call this skillful process *cognitive defusion*. Interestingly, recent studies have specifically found that when we become *fused* with our thoughts while emotionally activated, we lose our ability to discriminate the related specific emotion. Instead of effectively using our labeling skill (from the last chapter), fusion coactivates multiple (secondary) negative emotions (Plonsker et al. 2017). So, together with skillfully labeling your emotions, it's essential to get good at defusing from your thoughts. Below are two practices to start building your ability to defuse, decenter, and hold your position in the intersection of the present moment.

Defusing from Thoughts

Sometimes, the intensity of the language we use when we think and talk about our experience serves to increase the communication value (to others and ourselves). But there's a price to pay in terms of the symphony of other experiences that joins in to keep us feeling miserable. A great way to get in there and start disentangling these kinds of sticky thoughts is with a one-hundred-year-old defusion technique used in ACT.

LET'S PRACTICE: Thought Repetition

Look through your dashboards for any particularly sticky or emotionally evocative thoughts that showed up more than once (or that you know you believe strongly). For Jessica, it was *Nobody cares*. For Amy, it was *They're disrespecting me*. It's best to shorten the thought to a few words at most. Once you've identified the thought, allow it to roll around in your mind, and notice the pull of any emotions or bodily sensations as you do. Set a timer for two minutes and start repeating the thought *out loud*, over and over again as fast as you can. It's important that you do not stop until the two minutes are up. Ready? Go!

What did you notice about the impact and feeling of the words after you did this practice? This technique is a tried-and-true way to help you step back and defuse from the sticky meaning of the beliefs your mind offers up. In studies, thought repetition in this way has been shown to reduce both the believability and the ability of sticky thoughts to evoke related emotions (Masuda et al. 2009). After all, those phrases and thoughts are just a bunch of sounds that we infuse with meaning based on our past experiences.

Another way we get fused in our sticky thoughts is in how we speak out loud. "I'm such a _____," or "This is so _____." The way we speak our thoughts can make them feel like facts. So, a very simple strategy for defusing as we go about our life is to speak about our thoughts as thoughts, rather than as facts (Hayes and Smith 2005).

LET'S PRACTICE: Defused Speaking

Choose another thought from your dashboard forms. Say a short sentence or two about the thought. Notice how saying your thought or belief feels. Pause. Now before expressing the thought, begin by saying, "I'm noticing I'm having the thought…" Notice how you feel when you say it this way.

Can you see how adding this prefix to the way you speak about your thoughts (and your emotions, too) can help disentangle you a bit? This skill for communicating your thoughts can also be helpful when engaging others in difficult dialogues. When you highlight that your thought is exactly that, just a thought, it can help tamp down the antagonizing effects on others, as well as yourself.

Using a Mantra As an Anchor

A mantra is any group of words or sounds repeated. While the practice of using a mantra stems from various philosophies of Buddhism, a mantra is not a religious thing (unless you find that helpful). Mantras function as a tool for concentrating the mind and anchoring it in the presence of discomfort. Using such a word or phrase as an anchor is the core tool used in Transcendental Meditation practices, which have been found particularly effective for those experiencing severe anxiety symptoms (Orme-Johnson and Barnes 2014).

So, when you're feeling particularly triggered or agitated, this *closed focus* tool can also be used as an anchor while building the more *open focus* of mindfulness practice. The following Willingness Mantra serves two functions. First, it anchors your mind in the present moment when unhelpful emotion-driven thoughts are pulling on you. Most important, it reminds you of your intention to be caring and skillful with your emotions, rather than reactive. In the last chapter, you practiced putting your body through the willingness window with Willingness Hands; the next step is getting your mind on board and willing as well.

LET'S PRACTICE: Willingness Mantra

You may practice this mantra alone or add it to the Willingness Hands practice.

1. Identify the emotion label for your experience in this moment.

2. In your mind or aloud, say: "I am willing to have these thoughts and feelings of _____ in just this moment."

3. Repeat the mantra three to five times with an attitude of non-judgmental and kind allowing of your experience. Notice how you feel when you do.

LET'S PRACTICE: Awareness and Acceptance Mantra

Another helpful mantra for anchoring in an emotion storm is the Awareness and Acceptance Mantra (Linehan 1993b), introduced in chapter 6. As with any mantra you choose, you may use it during your day-to-day life, together with Willingness Hands, or during formal practice to help anchor your mind.

1. On the in-breath, say to yourself, "I am inhaling with awareness."

2. Notice where you are, what you see and hear around you, and any thoughts and feelings pulling on you.

3. On the out-breath, say, "I am exhaling with acceptance..." You are accepting things just as they are, in this moment.

4. Repeat three to five times.

Did you notice a difference in how you felt after these short practices? The great thing about these mini–mindfulness practices is that they can help you build the core mindfulness skills of redirecting attention and of acceptance of the present moment. These short practices are excellent choices for when you are out and about, tackling the stresses of adulting. Now, let's up your game a bit with some longer practices to build your skillfulness with thoughts over time.

Stepping Back from the Head Trip with Formal Practice

Formal meditation practice is where you can supercharge your ability to step back from thoughts and watch your mind do its thing. Meditation gives you a safe space to practice the essential skills of nonjudgmentally observing and redirecting to the now, over and over again. While committing to meditation can be tough at first, research has shown that it can improve mind wandering (Rahl et al. 2017) after just three short practices and mood after a few weeks (Winnebeck et al. 2017).

The cool thing about mindfulness meditation is that it acts as a sort of projection test from which you can discover how the contents of your mind are being projected onto the facts of the situation. In a projection test, a psychologist asks the person being assessed to tell a story about a drawing or inkblot on a card. From that story, the therapist extrapolates ideas about what the person is experiencing and projecting onto the card. Because, after all, it's really just a blob of ink on a card! This is what we're looking for in your mindfulness practice. What are you carrying inside you and projecting onto the facts as you practice?

Just Sitting with Thoughts

The short formal practices that follow are like exercising your mindfulness muscles so you can build the essential skill of stepping back from the head trips your mind offers up. Even if you can feel the pull toward avoidance, I really encourage you to at least give these following practices a try so you can build up your internal connections to a place where you can observe thinking as a process, rather than as factual happenings.

LET'S PRACTICE: Breath, Body, Sound Meditation

This meditation, introduced in chapter 5, is a great general practice to build into your routine. In this meditation, you are practicing moving your attention in a structured way, which is based on the most-studied mindfulness protocols. This practice will guide you to actively hold your attention on the physical sensations of your breath and body first and then to expand your attention to add awareness of sound.

Remember, minds time travel; bodies do not. This practice will help you build a foundation for anchoring in the body and then observing and redirecting attention to the present moment. By anchoring in the breath and body first, you are building the neural roadways of stepping out of the whirlwind of your mind habits and back to the place of the observer. Adding sound awareness helps balance awareness of self with awareness of the situation: what's happening inside the vehicle with what's happening outside. This practice will be very helpful in learning the *felt sense* of stillness and developing your ability to return to it when needed in your life.

LET'S PRACTICE: Beach Balls on the Water

This visualization will guide you to create a peaceful image while observing the process of thinking as it comes and goes. In the recording (at http://www.newharbinger.com/41931), you will be asked to observe and label each thought as it emerges. Each time a thought, image, memory, judgment, or worry arises, the practice is to imagine the thought as a beach ball that you gently release into the sea. This core ACT practice will help solidify your learning to look *at* your thoughts, rather than through them: to see thoughts as an activity of the mind, rather than facts in the present moment. Each time you release a beach ball, you are practicing *letting go* of thoughts.

LET'S PRACTICE: Listening to Thoughts for a Secret

I developed this practice while working with a client experiencing the most intense form of racing thoughts—hallucinations. His medication had not yet been prescribed, so he was hearing voices telling him all kinds of scary things. I asked him, "What are they saying? Let's listen." When he silently paused to listen to his thoughts, rather than generate them, he turned to me with wide eyes, "They stopped!"

When you're hooked into a debate in your head and your thoughts are racing, this skill can help slow them down a bit to give you the space you need to be more skillful. In this practice you are actively switching from *generating* thoughts—our usual thinking mode—to listening to your thoughts as if they are telling you an important secret.

Mind Warps: When Thought Passengers Go Rogue

By now you're getting the idea that the human mind is very prone to distorting information in the present moment. In traditional CBT, a number of "cognitive distortions" have been identified, which can contribute to amplifying emotions. We're all prone to these thinking errors. There's nothing wrong with you for having them. They're simply not helpful in objectively responding to the facts of a situation. Some of these types of *mind warps* are consolidated in the table on the next page. Learning to recognize when your mind offers them up can be extremely helpful in clueing you in when your thoughts are a less-than-accurate appraisal of the current facts. Learn them, know them, and check them for accuracy!

Table 9.1. *Common Mind Warps*

Mind Warps and Content	Typical Thoughts
All-or-none, black-and-white thinking: Extreme interpretations, such as "always," "never," "totally"	*I never get to...* *She always does this!*
Blaming (a type of judgmental thinking): Holding others responsible, "shoulding," faultfinding	*This is not okay!* *Not fair!* *They did this to me!*
Catastrophizing: Assuming the absolute worst outcome from the event	*This will be/is/was a disaster!*
Emotional reasoning: Mistaking feelings for facts	*If I feel this way, it must be true.*
Mind reading: Assumptions about what others are thinking based on their actions	*He's ignoring/disrespecting me!* *She thinks I'm stupid.*
Minimization or magnification: Dismissing some facts as irrelevant or giving greater weight to supporting evidence	*Yeah, but...* *It's not important.* *Just this once.* *That doesn't count.*
Overgeneralizing and time traveling: Generalizing present facts from the past or to future events	*If this happened before, then it will happen again.* *If it's happening now, it will always be happening.*
Personalizing: Relating outside events back to self as a causal agent	*I'm being punished for...* *Why is this happening to me?*

PAUSE. What types of mind warps showed up most frequently in your dashboards? On each dashboard you've completed, write down the mind warp that best matches your interpretation of events. You'll refer to these again later in your mindful-mastery practice plan.

What's Being Left Out? Checking the Facts

Mind warps as a whole tend to be extreme in nature: they pull you into the all-or-none space and heat up your emotions. Once you've recognized a mind warp, the next step is to start gently nudging your mind toward the more balanced interpretation. A good way to start is by asking: Is this thought 100 percent true? What might be a slightly less extreme, but also true, interpretation?

LET'S PRACTICE: Finding the Mind Warps

Review your dashboards to find the mind warps. Label them as such on the form. Next, ask yourself, "Was the thought I was having 100 percent true?" If the answer is no, write down the more balanced thought.

"Sure!" you may say. "Of course, I want to get to the objective thought." Ah, if only it were so easy, humans wouldn't get stuck in the many quagmires of disagreement and misunderstandings we do! To override our natural tendency to buy into what our mind tells us can often take a Herculean effort of asking ourselves, "What's being left out?" When the answer to the 100 percent question isn't getting you there, it's time to dig down deeper and check the facts!

LET'S PRACTICE: Checking the Facts

Choose one of the mind warps you identified from your dashboards that is still bugging you. Write down the facts and thoughts from this entry in your journal and practice the following steps inspired by Greenberger and Padesky (1995).

Step 1: Find the trigger thought. Review the thoughts and interpretations you had of the facts. Identify one specific thought related to a strong reaction to the facts and circle it.

Step 2: Find the passenger behind the thought. It's often not immediately clear why our thoughts and interpretations are triggering, so you may be tempted to dismiss or minimize your reaction. Before you do, let's get in there and take a deeper look at what underlying belief might have been triggering you. To do this, ask yourself the following questions, and write your answers in your journal. If this thought were true, what would it mean to me about:

- the other person, the situation, or the world in general?

- my life circumstances?

- me as a person and my value in the world?

As you review the answers to these questions, notice if you feel the pull of the emotion related to that event bubble up. If you feel a tug, tension, or your eyes water a bit, you may have a passenger!

Step 3: Validate the facts. Next, take a moment to self-validate. In your journal, make a list of all the evidence in your life that supports your thought or underlying belief. You might choose to use your validation statement to honor the painful emotions that come up as you identify the historical reasons this thought *feels* really true.

Step 4: Check the facts. Now comes the hardest part. Search beyond what your mind wants to believe for any and all evidence to the contrary. Ask: *What's being left out?* What might someone else who is observing the situation see? This is usually very difficult to do. Our mind is programmed to search for evidence to support our own beliefs. *And* there is almost always some evidence to the contrary of what we believe. In your journal, make a list of *all* the remotely possible evidence that does *not* support the thought.

Step 5: Find the balanced thought. Once you've completed that last brave move, compare the two lists. Summarize each side of the evidence so you have a more concise overview of both sides of the equation. From these summaries, apply the No Buts skill from chapter 6. Write down the first summary, write "and," and then write the second summary to find the balanced place of both-ness.

This core thinking skill is usually challenging at first. Remember how much we humans love being certain about our thoughts? Asking, *What's being left out?* like this asks you to step out of certainty and helps you stay open to alternative viewpoints and creative problem solving.

Practice tip for uncertainty thoughts. Some of the most distressing thoughts that your mind may offer are questions and doubts: *What's wrong with me? Why does he keep doing that? I don't know if I can do this!* But what you react to emotionally is actually the statement of the question or an underlying assumption behind the *I don't know* thought. If question-thoughts show up on your dashboards, change the questions into statements. For example, change, *What's wrong with me?* to *There is something wrong with me.* Change, *I don't know if I can* to *I can't.* Then check the facts for that thought. Lastly, "why" questions tend to suggest an underlying judgment. You don't question when something is going "right," right? So, check to see what the underlying judgments might be when you ask why.

Being Skillful with Judgments: Compassionate Reframing

Before wrapping up this chapter on thought skills, let's consider working with judgmental thoughts. When we're judging, we are, by definition, not accepting some aspect of the current situation, either inside or outside the vehicle. As a fundamental piece of mindful awareness, the nonjudgmental facet has been found to predict lower levels of depression, anxiety, and stress-related symptoms (Cash and Whittingham 2010). Thus, countering judgmental thinking is a worthwhile practice.

LET'S PRACTICE: Finding the Compassionate Reframe

Review your dashboards or reflect on a recent interaction where you were angry or annoyed and identify the judgmental thoughts. Go through the steps above again. This time, in step 4, search for a kinder, more compassionate interpretation. From the other person's perspective, why might it make sense that he or she is doing the thing that is offending you? Could that person be having a bad day? Could he or she have different information or past experiences leading to his or her particular behavior? Take a mental snapshot of how you feel before and after finding the more compassionate interpretation.

When you really get in there and imagine a less judgment-laden, more compassionate reason, that this person is behaving the way he or she is (or a situation is the way it is), you are highly likely to notice the tension in your body subside and the irritation decrease. So ultimately, the compassionate reframing, like all your skills, is not for the other person at all. It's for you! In this chapter, you learned the second step in effectively regulating and maintaining a flexible ETA system: how to *check* your thoughts. Once you have *validated* your emotions and *checked* your thoughts, the next step in skillfulness is taking *control* where you have it: in your actions!

CHAPTER 10

Taking Control of Your Actions: Change Skills

Forrest: *Lieutenant Dan! What are you doing here?*

Lieutenant Dan: *I'm here to try out my sea legs.*

Forrest: *But Lieutenant Dan, you ain't got no legs...*

Lieutenant Dan: *Yes....Yes, I know that.*

—From the movie *Forrest Gump*

Years after Forrest Gump asked fellow Vietnam vet Lieutenant Dan to be first mate on his shrimping boat, Lieutenant Dan showed up unexpectedly! In the 1994 film, Forrest is a compassionate and caring young man who, despite his intellectual disabilities, manages to push beyond his limitations to achieve success wherever he goes. On this sunny day in southern Alabama, as he coasts along on his dilapidated fishing boat, he catches sight of his wheelchair-bound friend, waiting for him on the dock.

We see the emotions of excitement and joy immediately spread across his face. His body tenses, and his shoulders rise with exhilaration as he waves frantically to his beloved friend. He can barely contain himself! In fact, he does not: the trigger-emotion-action impulse overwhelms him. He runs toward his friend, straight off the boat and into the water. So taken over by the thrill of reuniting, no one is left steering the boat as it crashes into the neighboring dock.

Although it doesn't seem quite so endearing when it happens to us, most of us can recount our own Forrest Gump moments. Can you recall a time when your emotions jumped up and grabbed you so fast and strong that you lost control of the vehicle? This chapter is about regaining control—in the only place we have it—in our actions!

The Emotion–Action Link

Of course, our actions may not feel in control when we're seized by a Forrest Gump moment. That powerful, biological pull of strong emotions does indeed make self-control more difficult. Each emotion pulls and pushes for an autopilot, hardwired behavioral reaction. Sadness and shame pull on us to withdraw and hide. Fear and anxiety tell us to run away and avoid. Anger pushes us to fight for what is just. When these emotions are *justified* for the facts of the situation, the related action tendency is often the effective thing to do. If you're walking down a dark alley at night and you see a person hiding in the shadows holding a weapon, running away is a darn good choice!

This chapter, however, is going to introduce skills for helping you self-regulate when either (a) the emotion is *not* justified for the facts of the situation, or (b) the emotion is justified, but you need to self-regulate to be effective in the service of your goals. Your actions are your most powerful ally in maintaining your mental health and building a life you love. So let's get started learning to use your actions to self-regulate!

The Power of Behavior

Move your arm to pretend you're lifting a weight, like you're doing a muscle curl. When you do that, it's not only your brain sending a message to your arm. Your arm is also sending a message to your brain.

Every action you take sends a message to the brain. The more often you do it, the stronger the connections become. This is the power of what is called *neuroplasticity*—the brain's ability, throughout life, to continue to grow new connections from the things you practice. In this way, your brain is constantly changing as you learn and *practice* new things.

The goal of the practices in this chapter is to build your connection to upregulating when you're feeling down and to downregulating when you're feeling agitated, anxious, or too wound up to be effective. The skills in this chapter are intended to help you gain a sense of behavioral control when emotions are high and to build your emotional resilience to stress using self-care.

You Got This: When You Need It *Now!*

Sometimes, you just need to get through a moment without making it worse. When you've been triggered and you feel a Forest Gump moment coming on, there are a few things you can do to hack into the ETA spiral and slow the emotion–action link to increase your *distress tolerance*. Distress tolerance is your ability to have and withstand difficult emotions. The following skills will help you bring down the emotion enough to get back on track. As with all the skills, it's a good idea to practice *before* you really need them so you're crystal clear on what to do. Remember, when stress is high and emotions get strong, *you will not want to use your skills!* So plan ahead. Let's practice.

Quick Fixes to Keep You from Losing Your Cool

When passengers are hijacking our mind and body, we get pulled into a full cascade of psycho-physiological reactivity. Our breathing gets shallow, we perspire, our muscles tense, and we can't think clearly; we're in full-blown autopilot! So sometimes, we need a short-term skill to get through a moment without making it worse by acting impulsively.

A good way to hack into the reaction is to use our physical sensations to change the messages being sent upstream to our brain. The following skills are adapted from DBT, which is a mindfulness-based treatment developed for severe emotion dysregulation. These skills will help you hack into your body chemistry so you can regain a sense of self-control. With practice, they can help you reduce the emotion phobia that keeps you hooked on the emotional habits that keep you stuck!

LET'S PRACTICE: Ice, Ice Baby

Rapidly shifting your body temperature can help override the physiological reactions to a trigger. I can't tell you how many times I've heard clients respond with, "Wow, that really worked!" when I coached them to use this skill.

Get some ice (or a bag of frozen food) from the freezer and put it in a plastic bag. Place it on your forehead. Next, hold your breath for thirty seconds. Put your complete attention into feeling the ice and holding your breath.

Doing this practice activates the *dive response* in your body, so your brain thinks you're underwater. It redirects essential blood flow to the brain and slows your heart rate (Khurana et al. 1980). You can't ruminate when your body thinks it's underwater! Try this skill next time you're panicking or freaking out before taking action.

LET'S PRACTICE: Slow and Easy, Paced Breathing

Your mind-body vehicle, like all vehicles, comes with an accelerator and a braking system. Within your central nervous system, there is the *sympathetic nervous system*, which is the accelerator. It gets activated when you need to get moving to run away from a threat. Your breaths are short, shallow (only into the chest, rather than the belly), and rapid. Your brake system is called the *parasympathetic nervous system* and kicks in when a threat has passed. This system is also called the "rest and digest" mode of your nervous system. It's related to the slow sigh of relief you make when stress has passed. Here too, the system is bidirectional, so you can hack into it by actively pacing your breathing.

In this skill video, you will practice pacing your breaths in order to activate the relaxation response. By slowing your breath, so that your exhale is longer than your inhale, you can start overriding the autopilot reactivity in your mind-body vehicle. Try it for yourself!

Notice how you feel after breathing in this way. This type of slow belly breathing hacks into your braking system to let your brain know that you are safe. I recommend practicing this skill throughout the day, when you're in the car, in meetings, or just hanging around. The more you practice this type of relaxed breathing, the more accessible it will be to you the next time you feel triggered.

Practice note. You may adjust the time to three and five seconds, or six and eight. The key is to make sure the exhale is longer than the inhale. You can also pair this practice with the Willingness Hands practice from chapter 8 to balance accepting emotions with changing reactivity.

LET'S PRACTICE: Holding Tight and Letting Go

Another great way to let go of a heightened emotional reaction is to recognize when the tension is creeping up in your body. Remember, your body is often sending you messages long before your mind starts to notice that you're getting upset. This skill will help you start recognizing when you're holding tight and then practice letting go.

In this video, you're going to actively practice tightening each muscle group (as listed below) related to emotions and then letting them soften. To practice, tighten each as tight as you can, and then as you release, say slowly in your mind, "Letting go." Hold the tension for about *ten seconds*, then let go, and take a moment to observe the difference in how you feel each time.

- Pull your shoulders up to your ears as if you're very stressed, hold, and then let go.

- Clench your fists and tighten your forearms, hold, and then let go.

- Furrow your brow as if you're pissed off, hold, and then let go.

- Clench your teeth, pushing your tongue on the roof of your mouth, hold, and then let go.

- Stretch your legs out, tensing your thighs, buttocks, and stomach, hold, and then let go.

Were you able to feel the distinct differences between holding and letting go? Letting go feels better, doesn't it? As with all the practices, skillfulness comes with repetition. So if you suffer from bodily symptoms of mood or anxiety, keep practicing! This skill will help you notice tension creeping in earlier in the ETA cycle and override the reactivity.

LET'S PRACTICE: Half-Smile, a Breath Mint for the Mood

Just as our emotions are hardwired in the body, they're also strongly connected to our facial expressions. If you think about it, the facial expressions of happy, sad, scared, angry, and disgusted are universally identifiable. No one has to teach us to recognize them. But when we're feeling upset, we may try to hide our emotion by stonewalling our facial expressions. Does this work? Let's check it out.

Did you notice how different it feels between trying to cover up your emotions versus gently allowing the corners of your lips to float up? Perhaps you noticed the natural sense of relief or a slight brightening of mood, as people have in research studies (Draft and Pressman 2012). The idea is not to plaster a fake smile on your face, particularly if your emotion is justified and it is a time and place where self-validation is in order. This tool is specifically for when you are in a place that's not ideal for exploring your emotions. I call this skill a breath mint for the mood because it will get you through when you're in a pinch but should *not* be used for ongoing emotional hygiene!

PAUSE. How were those exercises for you? Did you find these short-term skills helpful? Different people respond differently to different practices. Make sure to note the skills that worked best for you.

Opposite Action: No Emotion Driving!

Now that you have some skills to get you through a stressful moment, we're going to move to ones that will build increasingly longer periods of emotional balance. Making the slow turn toward regulating your ETA system means increasingly taking action to override the autopilot behavioral habits that keep you stuck.

As you've been collecting your dashboard forms (You are collecting them, right?), what is the most recurring emotion that shows up?

Do you notice particular behavioral avoidance reactions? Countering unhelpful emotions means engaging in actions that move the arrows in the ETA system in the opposite direction. So choose the emotion (or two) that you would like to work on, and get ready to make a commitment!

Is the Emotion Justified? To Act or Not to Act

Taking the action opposite to your emotion can feel pretty invalidating. Remember, the purpose of your emotions is to communicate important information about your needs. Particularly when emotions are stronger, it can feel like doing the opposite is downright fake, insincere, or even manipulative. So before using this skill, you'll want to figure out if the emotion is really justified and then the best course of action to be most effective.

Tying It All Together with Opposite Action

Let's tie together everything you've learned about being skillful. The infographic that follows guides you through the process of integrating your *validate* skills for emotions, your *check* skills for thoughts, and finally your *change* skills for your actions. This is the big-picture prescription for regulating your ETA system! No matter what emotion you're experiencing, the recipe for healthy emotion regulation is always the same! *Validate, check, change. Validate, check, change.* To help you remember the essential recipe for emotional self-care, let's do a quick practice.

PAUSE. Place your hands on your chest; say *validate*. Place your fingertips on your temples; say *check*. Point both index fingers forward like handguns; say *change*. I call this the *mindfulness Macarena*. I know, it's silly. *And* it will help you remember the essential steps!

Whether or not your emotion is justified for the facts of the situation, you're having it for a reason. Remember, the most recent research shows that emotion labeling and acceptance are both important features of emotion regulation (Kotsou et al. 2018; Torre and Lieberman 2018). So always begin with one of the *validation* skills (from chapter 8) to slow down, label, and practice *self-compassion or willingness* with your emotion. Once you've taken this essential step of honoring the emotion, you're ready to step into observe mode. See your thoughts as thoughts, rather than facts. Using your thought skills (from chapter 9), keep your thoughts in *check* from any mind habits or warps and *check the facts*. Is your emotion justified for the facts? If it's *not*, take *opposite action*! If your emotions *are* justified, then you may choose to use opposite action just until you figure out what values-consistent action is needed to get your needs met effectively.

Unlike the other skills you've been learning, this isn't one we can practice as a here-and-now exercise (unless you're feeling a strong emotion right now; if you are, you could jump in and practice the opposite action now and come back to reading later). But in most cases, you'll have to make a deal with yourself to schedule an opposite-action activity. Consider one of the emotions with which you're struggling. Below, you'll find a table of the most common emotions and their natural action tendencies. In the third column are the actions *opposite* to the natural tendencies. Find the category of emotion words that best fits your experience and make it a point to take one or more of the opposite actions in the week to come when you feel triggered or just stuck in the emotion.

Table 10.1. *Emotions and Their Action Tendencies*

Emotion Words	Action Impulse	Opposite Action
Sadness, alienation, disappointment, depression, grief	Slow down, withdraw, isolate, stay in bed, frown, slump, cry, be inactive	Get active. Do things you're good at or like. Pay attention to positives in your life. Take a hot or cold shower.
Fear, anxiety, dread, panic, worry, overwhelm	Run away, avoid feared situations, freeze, do controlling behaviors	Do what scares you. Approach. Approach, repeatedly.

Anger, irritation, frustration, annoyance, agitation, grumpiness	Attack (physically or verbally), stomp feet, slam doors or other things, speak in a loud voice, swear, criticize, complain	Kindly avoid. Behave kindly. Compassionately reframe.
Disgust, contempt, aversion, disdain, repulsion	Look away, clean, avoid eating or drinking, push away, grimace	Move closer. Take in. Do the opposite actions from anger.
Envy, begrudging, resentment	Reduce what other person has, sabotage, make the other person look bad, make yourself look better	Practice gratitude for what you have. Refrain from envy actions.
Shame, embarrassment, shyness, humiliation, mortification	Hide, cover up, bow head, overapologize	Out yourself: show what causes you shame (with safe people). Apologize or repair (if your action conflicts with your values).
Guilt, regret	Make amends, solve the problem, apologize, ask for forgiveness, overoffer	Do what makes you feel guilty. Out yourself (with safe people).
Love, caring, adoration, passion, affection	Care for, nurture, protect, touch, spend time together	Avoid and distract yourself from this person and any reminders. Do *not* follow the person on social media.

LET'S PRACTICE: Make a Commitment

In the coming week, schedule at least one activity that is opposite to the emotion you've been struggling with. Go through the steps of *validate, check, change,* and then stick to that commitment. Remember to set *levels* of commitment (optimal, acceptable, and passing) so you don't set yourself up for a pass-fail situation. Afterward, make sure to take note of your mood in your journal.

Taking the action opposite to an emotion *can* work to improve your mood right away. More important, it gets you in the skillful habit of building a life that is *not* driven by your emotion passengers. You are building a life skill of intentionally choosing where you want your life to go, rather than letting passengers decide.

Self-Care: Using Skillful M.E.A.N.S.: Meditation, Exercise, Abstinence, Nutrition, Sleep

No matter how skillful you are, if your vehicle is running sluggish due to illness or poor self-care, everything's going to feel harder! The biological machine you inhabit can obviously impact how strongly you react to the challenges of adulting and how powerful your passengers feel. So if you know you have a family history of mental health challenges or a current or past diagnosis (physical or mental), self-care is going to be extra essential for you! This section is about taking ownership of your mind-body vehicle to make it as resilient as possible along the bumpy roads of adulthood.

Self-care means different things to different people: it can be philosophical or preventative. Spending time with friends and loved ones, maintaining a healthy work-life balance, and attending to your soulful needs are all general steps you can take toward philosophical self-care. Here, I'm going to briefly discuss why it's important to take a preventative health approach to self-care: because of the impact of health behavior on stress, mood, and well-being.

When we get stressed out, it's easy, almost imminent, that we get pulled into poor health habits and low mood (Boardman and Alexander 2011; Mroczek and Almeida 2004). The stress–self-care cycle is self-perpetuating. Daily stress has been linked to poorer health behavior in college students and those suffering from depression (Dalton 2017). We've all been there. The stress hormones make us crave and eat more salty and sugary foods, we drink more alcohol, or we get less sleep and exercise. Before we know it, our mood is spiraling, and we just can't seem to correct course!

The science is clear: how we care for our body, and what we put in it, has a powerful influence on the effects of stress on our mood states and well-being. The good news is there's a lot we can do to promote our mood and psycho-physiological resilience to stress. Here is a quick rundown of some of the most powerful health behaviors and how they can support, or sabotage, the flexibility in your ETA system. Committing to and maintaining your health habits is tough, *and* here are the five pillars of healthy actions as skillful M.E.A.N.S. in self-care, which are long-term investments in your mental (and physical) health.

Meditation

It can't be said enough: in today's world of endless distractions, we're all in increasing need of some intentional "unplug" time to practice our mind discipline. Short mindfulness practices have been directly linked to less emotional reactivity and more willingness to engage in emotionally distressing tasks (Arch and Craske 2006; Erisman and Roemer 2010; Campbell-Sills et al. 2006). But if you need more encouragement, large-scale reviews have found that consistent practice is related to improvements in the brain in areas related to attention, introspection, and emotional processing (Hatchard et al. 2017). In choosing your preferred method of meditation, consider the degree and type of struggle you're working with. The most consistent evidence for the beneficial effects of mindfulness meditation for mental health have been found with depression, pain, smoking, and addictions (Goldberg et al.

2018). But for symptoms of severe anxiety or pronounced emotion dysregulation, using one of the mantras from chapter 9 or Paced Breathing from chapter 10 as an anchoring technique might be most effective (Orme-Johnson and Barnes 2014; Menezes and Bizarro 2015).

Exercise

Yes, we all know we need to exercise. Hey, I get it! If you're feeling like crap already, this can be really hard to do. Nonetheless, as a physical stressor, exercise actually raises the threshold required to activate the stress response (Viru and Viru 2004; Traustadóttir, Bosch, and Matt 2005). That means when you do cardio, your vehicle can tolerate more stress in your life, so you can keep tackling the stuff you need to do. Exercise improves both anxiety (Stonerock et al. 2015) and depressive disorders (Barbour, Edenfield, and Blumenthal 2007). It has also been found to reduce inflammation (Kohut et al. 2005), increase endorphins (Allen 2000), and promote the aforementioned neuroplasticity (Gleeson et al. 2011; Ernst et al. 2006), which creates antidepressant effects in the brain (Adlard and Cotman 2004; Russo-Neustadt et al. 2001).

Since you're reading this book, I'm guessing you are not elderly. If you're concerned about your physical abilities, naturally check with your doctor. As a rule of thumb, however, walking the dog around the block may be a great opposite action for depression. But if you want to seize the benefits of exercise, you have to get up and get sweating! Hit the treadmill or the bike for twenty to thirty minutes, three to five times per week, at 70 percent of your personal max capacity. This type of workout, practiced for three to five weeks, has been found to significantly reduce symptoms of anxiety and depression (Dunn, Trivedi, and O'Neal 2001; Dunn et al. 2005). As a moving meditation, yoga is also an excellent choice and allows you to double dip your exercise with your mindfulness practice. Studies have found yoga to improve a wide variety of stress and mood symptoms (Pascoe and Bauer 2015).

Abstain (from Drugs and Alcohol)

Drugs and alcohol can make regulating your emotions *a lot* more difficult. If you have an anxiety or mood disorder, you're twice as likely to develop a substance use issue (Conway et al. 2006). And vice versa: if you abuse drugs and alcohol, you're twice as likely to suffer from a mood or anxiety disorder (Quello, Brady, and Sonne 2005). If you're already struggling to regulate your vehicle, just be mindful of how much you consume. According to the U.S. Department of Health and Human Services, moderate alcohol consumption is considered just one drink per day for women, two for men (one drink is one 5-oz. glass of wine, 12-oz. beer, or 1.5 oz. of hard liquor). Three drinks in a single day or more than seven per week is considered "heavy" or "at risk" for women. For men, it's four drinks per day or fourteen in a week (2015).

Nutrition and Diet

If you're noticing that your symptoms of anxiety or depression make you feel like you're "wired and tired" at the same time, your thinking is foggy, or your energy is just zapped, heads up! This section is important. The emerging science of our "second brain"—the gut's microbiome, the community of bacteria, fungi, and viruses—sheds light on the importance of our diet in boosting the resilience of our vehicle.

We now know that 60 percent of our dopamine (the "happy chemical") and 90 percent of our serotonin (the "contentedness chemical") is in our gut (Mayer et al. 2014). Unfortunately, our modern diets of processed, simple-sugar-laden foods (and overuse of steroid and antibiotic medications) contribute to imbalances in the microbiome and wreak havoc on our gut's ability to absorb nutrients effectively (Mayer 2016). Researchers in this emerging science are finding that "There is mounting evidence linking the [gut] microbiome to risk for psychiatric illness, particularly depression and anxiety" (Liu 2017, 656). The good news is a few dietary changes might help. This section is not comprehensive but includes just a few tips to begin rebalancing the bugs in your gut so you can get those nutrients up and into your brain!

Reduce refined sugar and processed foods. Our favorite junk foods may give us a quick boost, but they increase the stress hormone cortisol (DiNicolantonio et al. 2017), which has been linked to brain cell death and depression (Sapolsky 2003). Sugar feeds candida (yeast) overgrowth (Han, Cannon, and Villas-Boas 2011), which has been proposed to underlie chronic fatigue syndrome (Cater 1995). If you crave sweets all the time, feel exhausted, foggy in the cockpit (even after ample rest), or get a lot of infections, you might want to ask your doctor about candida. Check your tongue for a white coating. Nail fungus or weird skin rashes may also suggest an overgrowth. Candida in your gut can lead to permeability in the gut lining, leading to food allergies and making it difficult to absorb the nutrients your brain needs (Mayer 2016).

Carb up with plants. A diet rich in *complex* carbohydrates (including dark breads, oatmeal, and whole grains) may promote resilience during times of stress. One cool study found that high-stress responders fared worse on a stress test while consuming a diet high in protein but low in carbs. They showed improved stress reaction and lower depression following a diet high in complex carbs and lower in protein (Markus et al. 2000). So if you notice you react strongly to stress (and aren't gluten intolerant), complex carbs might help.

Don't forget your veggies! They up your fiber content, which will keep your gut moving and get toxins out. But certain veggies are extra important to keep your gut healthy. Artichokes, dandelion greens, onions, and garlic all have prebiotics, the food for probiotics, which are essential for keeping the bugs in balance.

Include probiotic-rich foods. In a recent analysis of ten studies, it was shown that in those reporting mild-to-moderate anxiety or depressive symptoms, probiotic supplementation led to significant improvements in symptoms (Ng et al. 2018). Yogurt and fermented foods, like sauerkraut and kefir, are an excellent source of probiotics.

Eat lean proteins. Fish oils and other foods containing high amounts of omega-3 fatty acids contribute to a protective layer around brain cells called myelination (McNamara and Carlson 2006). Myelination is like insulation around brain cells that improves the clarity in the connections. Think of this as reducing the static in your brain! There's been a lot of research on the effects of omega-3s on mood and anxiety, which suggests they're helpful in managing mood (Soh et al. 2009). Hardboiled eggs are also excellent and convenient little omega-3-rich protein bombs.

Turkey is also a great choice because it increases L-tryptophan, which is the precursor to serotonin. Under stress, serotonin neurons are more activated and thus in need of more serotonin. In studies where the subjects' L-tryptophan was depleted, significant increases in depressive symptoms followed (Markus et al. 2000).

Sleep Habits

Irregular and poor sleep habits are one of the most important contributors to emotion dysregulation and psychological problems. According to a recent review of the abundant research, poor "sleep may affect the ability to identify an emotion as problematic, choose an appropriate emotion regulation strategy, and implement that strategy in an effective way" (Palmer and Alfano 2017, 14). So it's essential to take simple precautions to minimize dysregulation due to poor sleep quantity or quality. Make a commitment to follow a consistent sleep-wake cycle. Dim the lights ahead of sleep time, get in bed at least thirty minutes before you need to fall asleep, reduce caffeine later in the day, and, as best you can, get at least seven to eight hours.

When Illness Makes Mood and Motivation Harder

Naturally having physical ailments can make self-care even more important and more challenging. Problems such as chronic pain, type 2 diabetes, polycystic ovary syndrome, autoimmune diseases, and irritable bowel syndrome are highly correlated with increased mental health challenges (Bland 2017). The related mood and anxiety symptoms often land sufferers in the therapist's office. But there might be some additional steps you can take to make sure you're getting the full picture of your mind-body health.

If you're noticing that you check the boxes for many of the physical symptoms of mood and anxiety, you may want to work with a professional health practitioner to help you get started on some of your self-care goals. It can be tough going, though, to find well-trained integrative specialists because the fields of psychiatry, nutrition, and health are still so segregated. There's a lot of overlap between the symptoms of the above-noted syndromes and mental health, so you may find yourself running from doctor to doctor without getting any answers!

I encourage you to look for a *functional medicine* doctor. These practitioners test and treat your mind and body as an integrated system, not just the individual parts and symptoms. Just as this book has been getting at the psychological *root causes* of mood and motivation, a functional medicine doc will do the same for your physical symptoms. These holistic doctors seek the root cause by testing things like your gut microbiome, food allergies, and genetic variations, which might be off the radar of a traditional Western MD. Mark Hyman, medical director at Cleveland Clinic's Center for Functional Medicine, says, "Functional medicine is the future of conventional medicine" (Hyman 2009). So do some research to find a functional MD or a certified naturopath who will take a holistic, individualized approach to your well-being.

If self-care was a value you identified, I hope you found this brief introduction to preventative self-care helpful. If you'd like to dive deeper into promoting your mind-body health, check out Dr. Frank Lipman's book *How to Be Well: The 6 Keys to a Happy and Healthy Life* (2018). At the end of the day, just as we must maintain all the things we cherish in our lives, it's up to you to maintain your mind-body vehicle. Take care of your vehicle, and it will take you a lot further, in a much more comfortable ride!

This chapter has been about changing your actions to influence your mood and motivation. Ultimately, the prescription for a skillful *you* is listening to and *validating* your emotional (and physical) experiences, stepping back to *check* your thoughts, and then *changing* your (re)actions! This section of the book is your resource for practicing and maintaining healthy flexible ETA system regulation. Next up is learning to use your skills with others and developing your Mindful-Mastery Practice Plan.

PART IV

SUCCESSFUL YOU: MAINTAINING COMMITMENT TO YOURSELF AND OTHERS

CHAPTER 11

Sharing the Road with Other Drivers

If you're frustrated because you're not getting what you want, stop for a second: Have you actually flat-out asked for it? If you haven't, stop complaining. You can't expect the world to read your mind. You have to put it out there.

—Sophia Amoruso, *#Girlboss*

Becoming an emotional grown-up is about more than just working skillfully with your own internal discomfort. I don't need to tell you that a huge proportion of our triggers comes from our interactions with other people. The skills you've been learning represent three-quarters of your skillfulness: *validating* your emotions, *checking* your thoughts, and *changing* your actions. So that part's on you!

The other quarter is being skillful in getting the change and support you need from others. And, ultimately—sorry to say—that's on you, too. Things get extra complicated when you're out there dealing with other people because now you also have to be skillful with *their* passengers. How do you negotiate the unpredictable terrain of the passenger-driven actions of other people and still get your own needs met? In this chapter, you'll learn how to apply your skills to do just that. This chapter is about effective interpersonal assertiveness.

Choosing Whose Discomfort

If you want to be happy and achieve the awesome things you want to get done, maintaining good relationships is essential. Unfortunately, sometimes we burn out our relationships or get burned out because we have trouble setting limits or asking for what we need skillfully. Healthy, sustainable relationships require a balance between the needs of each party: knowing when to ask and when to say no. Maintaining this balance is challenging because asking and saying no are uncomfortable. Whenever we ask for something or say no to another person's request, it demands that we be skillful with (a) a moment of uncertainty and possible disappointment and (b) the discomfort we impose on the other person when we ask.

Think about it for a second. Imagine you're sitting across from me and you need a pen that sits on the table between us. In this situation, there is a decision being made of *who* will take on the discomfort. If you ask me to pass you the pen, as you tolerate the uncertainty of the outcome, there are two possible results: (a) I can pass you the pen, thus choosing to take on the discomfort myself, relieve yours, and earn your approval, or (b) I can say no, and thus I am choosing your discomfort but have to tolerate your disappointment. Asking is difficult because of the vulnerability. Saying no is difficult because saying yes is rewarded (for example, with a smile or a thank-you), but saying no is punished (for example, with a frown or an "Oh really? C'mon!").

This simple pen example holds true in all the large and small ways we either pull comfort to our own side (when we ask others to listen and attend to our needs) or offer comfort to another (when giving our attention, listening, and meeting the needs of the other person). Too often, unfortunately, we get stuck in the double bind of whose discomfort to choose and error toward one side or the other. When we choose our own needs (and comfort) too often, it can burden the strength of the relationship. When we choose the relationship (the other person's comfort) too often, it can lead to resentment and feeling drained by our relationships.

Week after week, Amy's autopilot emotional habits drove her straight into this double bind. When she was amped up to get something done, she'd go full steam ahead, with just one aim in mind: "Getting shit done!" As she said, "Sometimes it's just hard to have patience for the BS." Her tendency to lean too hard on her side of the dynamic had obvious consequences, like when she got so preoccupied with her creativity and relationship goals that she lost sight of her work responsibilities and got fired. In her relationships, the lack of balance frequently led to arguments and misunderstandings because she would lose sight of the needs of the other person. These oversights would leave Amy with a carload of guilt passengers and endlessly working to repair the resulting shrapnel damage. "Yeah," she said, "it's like I'm constantly bringing doughnuts," referring to how she frequently tried to make up for these less-than-glorious moments.

PAUSE. Have you ever noticed that sometimes you feel like you're always doing the listening and offering in some relationships, which leaves you drained? On the other hand, are there some relationships where you may be taking the lion's share of the comfort position?

What's Most Important?

Have you ever found yourself wondering, *Am I right to ask for this?* or *Can I say no?* Amy would ask herself these questions, but because she was so focused on her own values and goals, she would frequently miss the bigger picture. When you're deciding whether to ask or say no to a request, you have to ask yourself: What's most important? Are my needs and values the priority? Or is it more important to put my energy into the relationship? In the table that follows (adapted from DBT) you will see the factors to consider to help you decide. When considering whether to push for your own agenda or pull back and go into listening and accepting mode, each factor should give weight to your decision.

Table 11.1. *Choosing Whose Discomfort: Factors to Consider*

Your Comfort: When to Ask or Say No	The Other's Comfort: When to Not Ask or Say Yes
You have more authority, or the request is appropriate to the relationship.	You have less authority, or the request is not appropriate to the relationship.
You are generally a giver in the relationship and tend to do things for yourself.	You have asked a lot or said no often in the relationship.
The relationship is strong and loving.	The relationship is tenuous.
The timing is good (person is not stressed at the time).	The timing is bad (person is stressed).
The outcome is important to your goals and values.	The outcome is not so important to your goals and values.

PAUSE. Consider a request you need to make or one to which you would like to say no. In the table above, add up the factors in each column that apply to your relationship with the other person. If you have more on the left, the more firmly you may hold to your needs. If you have more on the right, choose to lean toward the other person's needs.

Making Your Way in Traffic: Prioritizing Others

Being a good friend, partner, or even an amicable colleague is about more than just a transactional exchange of doing or not doing, asking or not asking. Solid relationships are built on a foundation of trust and caring. Amy was having problems in her relationships because she missed this important piece. The connection comes from how you respond to others when they need your support or have a different viewpoint, not just from how much you do for them. The trust comes when you learn to attend to them the same way you've been learning to attend to yourself. Now that you know how to be skillful with your own emotions (with willingness, compassion, and validation), can you see how this is also the most effective way to connect with others?

Have you ever found yourself caught in a difficult dialogue with someone where emotions were escalating and reasoning wasn't helping? You may have tried to make that person understand your viewpoint and vice versa. But it can feel like a futile battle as you try everything to stomp out the flickering flames of disagreement and emotion! You may have tried to focus on the positive, examine the pros and cons, problem solve for solutions, justify and rationalize, explain, compare, or *anything* to get to an understanding and the emotions to calm down! So, does it work? The unsatisfying answer is…sometimes. The question is, Why doesn't it work all the time? Well, as you've learned, when something's important to you and emotions are strong, the skill needed to defuse that trigger is radically different from logic.

Consider the reverse. Can you recall a time when you wanted someone to understand something important to you, but you didn't feel heard? If you know this frustration, you also know that your impulse is usually to react in some version of two alternatives. Either you try to amplify your argument (people yell when they don't feel heard), or, when this fails, you just shut down and give up (a behavior will stop if it is not reinforced). Neither of these produces skillful communication.

You probably know from your own experience that when communicating is important, efforts from the other party to dissuade or reason away your perspective and emotions are not effective. His or her attempts may momentarily silence you but have not truly changed your viewpoint and feelings. When things are getting tense or it's time to choose the relationship over your own needs, the skill you need is different. The skill you need is mindful listening and validation.

When the Relationship Is Most Important

Just as when you're being skillful with your own emotions, validation is the lubricant for skillful communication. Validation is active acknowledgment of the presence of difficulty (in yourself or someone else) without trying to change anything. "Wait a second!" Amy demanded, "How can I validate something if I disagree with it?" Remember, validation is *not* agreement, cheerleading, or approval. Validating the other person's perspective is simply finding the place where what the other person is feeling or thinking makes sense. Your job is to compassionately consider how the other person might be getting hijacked by a passenger and caught in an ETA loop.

Steps for Mindful Listening

To build more trust in her relationships and ultimately stop having to always "bring the doughnuts," Amy practiced the following steps in my office before using them with others. You may ask a trusted friend to help you role-play the following steps so that you can practice your mindful listening skills.

Step 1: Notice your own reaction. During a conversation, take note if your mind begins to wander off to what you want to say next. Stay present and anchor your attention in physical sensations, like your bottom in the chair or feet on the floor.

Step 2: Be compassionately curious. If you notice judgmental thoughts creeping up about that person's viewpoint, causing growing feelings of anger, frustration, or even anxiety, you might validate the BAH (biological factors, anyone might feel that way, or historical passengers) for the other person. Could the other party be under more stress, sleeping poorly, or something else? Would you feel that way if the shoe were on the other foot? Or maybe a historical situation is causing a vulnerable passenger on this issue.

Step 3: Compassionately reframe judgments. Use your compassionate reframe skill from chapter 9. Find a place where you may truly find compassion for the person's perspective and emotions. Sometimes this isn't so easy to do! When you really can't understand where he or she is coming from, let the person know you care by asking for more information (for example, say "Help me understand," or "Tell me more so I can better understand").

Step 4: Communicate understanding. Communicate understanding in both what you say and how you say it!

- *Use body language*: Lean in and maintain eye contact (no eye rolling).

- *Project a kind voice tone*: The tone of your voice often has more impact on others than anything you are saying. Make sure there is no sarcasm or harshness in your tone.

- *Express verbally*: Say, "I can understand why you feel this way," or "It makes sense from your viewpoint."

Over time, as Amy practiced this skill in her relationships, she noticed that others didn't react as strongly to her as they used to. As you practice more mindful, compassionate listening in your relationships, you're likely to notice this too. You're also likely to find that you too feel better when communicating in this way. When we offer compassion and validation to another, we are once again letting go of being right in the service of being effective. At the end of the day, it's not really for the other person, but for you! When you practice, you win on two fronts. You are letting go of carrying the tension of judgment, and you make an important investment in the relationship. This investment sets the stage for more effectively getting the support and connection you need in the future. Imagine how much more smoothly difficult communications could be negotiated if we were all so skillful rather than reacting on autopilot from past experience.

Holding Your Own: Prioritizing Yourself

Sophia Amoruso's assertion in the quote at the beginning of the chapter, "You can't expect the world to read your mind. You have to put it out there," is a frustratingly simple truth. But it's also important to put it out there *skillfully*. A lot of the time, because of the negativity bias in our mind, we focus on what we don't want rather than what we do want. All too often we know we want to feel different about a situation, but we're not clear about what *exactly* we want.

Getting Clear About Your Needs

Nina frequently failed to ask for help when appropriate because she often felt others asked too much. She didn't want to impose, or worse, to elicit the type of smothering she felt in childhood. Nina's difficulty stemmed from her belief that asking was equivalent to smothering. She expressed her frustration, "I feel like I'm just out there floundering at work. My boss gives me this project and expects miracles!" But like many of us, she wasn't clear about what she actually wanted from people at work.

An important key to getting your needs met from others is identifying specifically and behaviorally what *actions* you would like them to take that might make you feel the way you want to feel. Clear communication is good for everyone. When we ask *specifically* and *behaviorally*, it actually reduces the discomfort of uncertainty for others. You're doing them a favor by giving them a sense of certainty about their ability to meet your needs. People feel good when they can check the box and say to themselves, "Done!"

Nina and I explored her specific needs and what actions her boss or more senior colleagues might take to help her feel more supported. "Well, I guess it would be nice to have regular times to check in and ask questions," she confessed. "But isn't that asking a lot?" When we counted the factors to consider (from table 11.1) related to asking for regular meetings, we found that most of the factors on the left were true. Asking was indeed appropriate to the relationship, she mostly did things for herself, and the outcome was clearly in line with her value of building more authenticity into her life. She could find an appropriate time. While the strength of the relationship was still in question, regular meetings would likely improve that factor as well. Now it was time to take the skillful steps in asserting herself.

Steps to Effective Assertiveness: The VAR Skill

Once you've checked the factors to consider and specifically and behaviorally identified what you need, the key to skillful assertiveness is to apply a balance of your validation skills with your change skills with the other person. Below are the steps for what I call the *VAR skill*: validate, assert (specifically and behaviorally), reinforce.

Step 1: Validate the other person's perspective. Start by putting yourself in the other person's shoes. Consider and acknowledge the discomfort you may be imposing. People are more willing to do things they feel are acknowledged as difficult, rather than expected or for which the difficulty is minimized.

For Nina, this meant simply validating how busy her supervisor must be and asking if it would be inconvenient for them to meet on a regular basis. When it's time to ask something of someone (or say no), as much as possible, start with a validation statement: "I know you are super busy, so I hate to bother you," "I can understand where you are coming from on this," or just a simple "I hear you."

Step 2: Assert, specifically and behaviorally. If you can't see it or count it, you're not being clear enough. State your request or your decline, *specifically* and *behaviorally*. This can be the hardest part because we feel awkward and anxious about being so direct. We waiver, speak around the issue, suggest, or infer. But very often, we don't come right out and state, "May I have?" or "I cannot do that." Nina and I role-played with her directly asserting her specific request out loud. If saying no, don't just describe how you feel about doing it, but validate the inconvenience and actually say no.

Step 3: Reinforce: What's in it for them? Remember, a behavior is reinforced when it leads to a reward or avoids a discomfort. The goal here is to help the other person see how the request you're making is a win (or avoidance of a loss) for them. Tell them what's in it for them. Nina was pretty clear on this. She honestly believed she would perform better at her job if she had regular contact and the opportunity to get clarification on her projects.

The reinforcement might be a simple exchange, "If you do this for me, I will do this for you." Or, if the relationship is a strong one, you may simply tell the person how much it would help you for him or her to help you out. When saying no, you might consider an alternative smaller compromise if that works for you.

Practice tip. Be extra careful not to accidentally punish the behavior change you're trying to get. Sometimes, when the person tries to do something we need but fails to meet our expectation, we respond with complaints or criticisms. Make sure to reward small approximations to the goal. Express gratitude for the effort before reasserting.

PAUSE. Again, consider a request or decline you have been considering. In your journal, write a mini-script for how you can use VAR: validate, assert, reinforce. Practice this skill with small asks and declines to get the hang of it and build your sense of self-efficacy.

When the Relationship Is the Value

Being in love can be one of the greatest sources of joy and content-ment—and misery—in our adult lives. When they're healthy, our romantic relationships can contribute to life satisfaction and well-being, and even buffer against the effects of stress (Kiecolt-Glaser and Wilson 2017). But problems in our relationships can exacerbate symptoms of depression, anxiety, and substance abuse (Gable and Impett 2012). We can, quite literally, become "madly in love."

A huge part of Jessica's difficulties transitioning into college life was that her boyfriend lived out of town. Her romantic relationship was a value she held above all others. She would go out of her way to be loving and supportive. She would drive to see him, do kind things, and generally try to be "an awesome, fun, and easygoing girlfriend." Sounds great, right? What could possibly go wrong with this agenda? (Cue the ominous music.)

When Good Intentions Are Ineffective

Things can get confusing when we're acting on our values, as Jessica and Amy were, and somehow, we're still not being effective in our relationships. Jessica was getting increasingly triggered as her boyfriend seemed to be less and less available to hang out on video chat or make the drive to see her. The more aloof he became, the more Jessica doubled down on her loving and supportive valued actions.

What was going wrong here? We can also get hijacked by our pleasant emotion passengers! As we cling to good feelings and push away difficult feelings, we often fail to do what is most effective for the demands of the facts of the situation. Although Jessica's actions (bringing dinner, driving to see him, and so forth) were certainly in line with her relationship values, her actions were less and less about being effective toward pursuing her goal (maintaining the relationship) and more and more about clinging to her love passenger and settling down her loneliness and anxiety passengers. Jessica was caught in the classic "overofferer" cycle and failing to assert her own needs with her boyfriend.

In every interaction with other people, we are in some way teaching them what they can expect or ask of us. They learn from how we respond, in all the many nuanced ways, to the pushes and pulls on each other's boundaries. The very first thing you learned in this book was that humans will automatically and naturally do more of what feels good and less of what uncomfortable. So if you want to increase a behavior in others, you can influence their actions in two ways: either reward the actions or reduce their discomfort. Jessica was being ineffective because, as she was reacting to her own passengers, she was failing to set limits in a way that let her boyfriend know what would work for the longevity of their relationship.

Setting limits in our relationships isn't just about asking and saying no. We set limits in all the subtle ways we reward or punish (consciously or not) the behavior of those around us. "I'm not playing those stupid games! That's being manipulative. I want my relationship to be authentic," Jessica retorted when we explored how she might be reinforcing (or supporting) behavior she didn't want. But by doubling down on her loving and supportive actions, regardless of his behavior, she was no longer reinforcing the actions she wanted. Jessica may have hoped that her boyfriend would just benevolently recognize how generous she was being. But because humans by nature habituate (get used to things), he was naturally coming to take these things for granted. Perhaps more important, she was denying him another source of reinforcement: allowing him the space to start missing her so she could then reduce his discomfort with her presence!

PAUSE. Have you ever been hijacked by the love passenger? Have you ever had to choose between doing what felt authentic and loving versus setting a limit in the service of being effective for the longevity of the relationship?

When the relationship is the value, it's very easy to confuse committed actions toward our values with more subtle underlying passenger-driven actions. Sometimes, even when we're acting on our values, we have to step back, do a double take, and ask, Is what I'm doing working? So we revisited this question. "Remind me, what is the value again?" I asked. "To have a loving supportive relationship, of course!" To help her maintain and keep that relationship, I helped her to clarify. "As you behave according to this value, what do *you* need, specifically and behaviorally, to feel you are on track?" I asked. And so, Jessica began the process again in asking herself: *What do I need (specifically and behaviorally)?* She had to check the factors and then: validate, assert, reinforce.

When Villagers and Castles Comingle

From the beginning of this journey, you've been asked to consider how you relate to your internal experience. Are you more like a castle or a village dweller? Do you value your independence and tend to minimize or push away discomfort? Or are you more of a feeler and thrive upon and seek more deeply connected relationships? As you have seen, both modes have their strengths and their vulnerabilities.

As you've reflected on these qualities in yourself, it's highly likely that you also began considering these traits in your relationships. There's one last thing you should know about the castle and village relationships: each tends to attract the other! In village mode, we tend to strive so intensely for connection that we overlook the small invalidations from the castle dweller of our affections at first. All we see is the shine of their walls and someone who seems to have it all together. Villagers frequently overoffer to gain entry into the castle walls and fail to assert their own needs. Meanwhile, our independent castle dwellers are thinking, *This is great! She or he wants all the same things I do!* or *I can save this sensitive soul!*

Over time, each tends to elicit more of the qualities of the other as the relationship becomes closer. That is, when castle peeps pull up their walls to shut out difficult internal experience, it is often perceived as lack of empathy and inadvertently elicits an increase in intensity from the villager. Conversely, as the villager in the relationship experiences and expresses strong emotions, her castle partner is more likely to pull up her walls! Castle dwellers aren't as in touch with their emotions, so they respond to the emotions of others in the same way they respond to their own.

If you notice yourself go into one mode or the other in your relationship, take note! When you feel your castle walls go up as stonewalling or defensiveness, practice your compassion and validation skills. If you sense your inner villager getting panicky or critical because you feel banished from the castle, use your self-compassion and regulation skills first. Then, when the factors to consider are in your favor, gently inquire and validate your partner's difficulty as you ask, specifically and behaviorally, for the connected attention you need.

CHAPTER 12

Shifting from Autopilot to Mindful-Mastery

I can feel guilty about the past, apprehensive about the future, but only in the present can I act. The ability to be in the present moment is a major component of mental wellness.

—Psychologist Abraham Maslow

You're a ROCK STAR! You've come a long way! Wow! Reaching this last chapter has been a real journey of self-discovery and commitment for you. By now you've come to see that the universal laws of nature can often conspire to derail *all* of us humans. Sometimes our passengers show up as symptoms of difficult emotions or negative mind chatter. Other times it's more difficult to see the passengers. All we see are the external behaviors in reaction to the passengers, which keep them quiet but derail our happiness and success. If there's one big takeaway for you as you continue on your path beyond adulting, it is this: there's nothing wrong with you for having those uncomfortable thinking and feeling passengers! They can certainly make it more challenging to be effective in life. *And,* when you practice turning your mindful attention toward them and use your skills to validate your emotions, check your thoughts, and control your actions, they will have *a lot* less power.

By this point, you can also see that human beings will naturally and automatically revert to rigid habitual modes. So you need to set yourself up for success by making sure you are crystal clear on your unique auto-pilot habit patterns, the kinds of situations that trigger them, and the skills to activate when they do. In this final chapter, you're going to pull it all together into one succinct action plan for you to maintain mind-ful-mastery through and beyond adulting. Here you'll be summarizing the patterns from your dashboards and linking them to the skills you found most helpful.

Coping Ahead: Being Prepared to Override Autopilot

We all want to be more skillful—until those life triggers are up and on us. When first starting out, it's almost always the case that when I ask clients if they used their skills or considered which ones they might have used, the response is the same, "No! I was freaking out," or "I guess I forgot."

Assuming you're not simply being willful (and I'm guessing you're not if you got this far), there are two reasons for not using your skills when you need to apply them. The first reason is because you're still building your mastery. Like all skills, it's only with repetition over time that we *internalize* the steps for being skillful and what it feels like in our body when we do. If you've ever learned to play an instrument, you know that feeling of having to fumble through the process of playing a piece over and over again before it becomes natural. As you continue learning to mindfully tune your mind-body vehicle, it will take main-taining your commitment over time before it starts to feel more natural.

A second reason we fail to use our skills when needed is because, once internalized, the practices have to be *generalized* to a variety of different contexts. That's why Jessica had phone coaching as part of her treatment plan. It's a lot easier to assume Willingness Hands or do Paced Breathing when you're sitting at home than when the poop hits the fan in your life! It's important to practice your skills in as many places as you can so you can flexibly deploy them wherever you are. But because I can't be there to phone-coach you, I'm going to give you a tool to make sure you are crystal clear on your autopilot patterns and to make a plan for skillful coping when they happen.

Getting Clear on Your Pattern(s)

As you've been collecting your dashboards and building your mindful awareness of the relationship between events, what patterns emerged? Remember, emotional habit patterns emerge because they *function* to help you feel more good or less bad in some way *and* are happening repeatedly. So keep a sharp eye out for particular thought or action habits that might function (whether intentionally or not) as a way to reduce or avoid short-term discomfort. If you find a pattern where the thing you do or way you are thinking is getting in the way of you moving toward your goals and values, *bingo*! That's a pattern to take note of!

PAUSE. If you've collected *all* twelve dashboards and you're still having trouble seeing a pattern, grab the detailed Steps for Identifying Your Patterns sheet at http:///www.newharbinger.com/41931.

Shifting from Autopilot to Mindful-Mastery

It's time to set yourself up for success by linking your autopilot patterns with skillful alternatives in your Mindful-Mastery Practice Plan! In this section, you're going to build your personalized prescription for your emotional self-care in maintaining a healthy, flexible ETA system. If you found more than one pattern, you may want to make an additional practice plan for each pattern or trigger to help you stay clear on how to be most skillful. You will find the downloadable Mindful-Mastery Practice Plan worksheet at http://www.newharbinger.com/41931. To help you get an idea of how it all comes together, let's take a look at which skills Jessica, Nina, and Amy chose for their mindful-mastery plans.

Patterns and Practices for Village Dwellers: Jessica

Jessica began her journey struggling with desperate feelings of loneliness and abandonment, which were impacting her school performance and romantic relationship. As you have seen, this sensitive village girl had a very hard time attending to anything else in her life when her loneliness passengers showed up. The simple fact of being alone triggered her ETA (emotions, thoughts, actions) regulator into a whole cascade of intense physical sensations, mind warps, and action impulses. She was under-regulated. She chose skills that helped her self-regulate some of the intensity in order to be more effective toward her true-north goals.

If you've been relating mostly to Jessica's high sensitivity and tendency to have difficulty self-regulating, you might find the same skills she chose helpful in your life. As you can see in her mindful-mastery action skills, she chose to include two of the "when you need it now" change skills from chapter 10: Ice, Ice Baby (or taking a shower or bath) and Paced Breathing. These helped her reduce some of the secondary physical and emotional reactivity to her primary emotion (loneliness). Once she was able to build her distress tolerance to loneliness, her skills objective was to increase her *willingness* to use *self-compassion* and *self-validation*, rather than overrely on her reassurance-seeking habit. She would practice her other skills to help her hold onto the center and maintain her commitments to her values: creative writing for school and balancing her limits with her boyfriend.

Table 12.1. *Jessica's Mindful-Mastery Practice Plan*

TRUE NORTH: 1. Maintaining healthy relationships, 2. Creativity
FACTS: Time alone, need to do homework

AUTOPILOT	MINDFUL-MASTERY
EMOTIONS: Loneliness, anxiety (heart pounding, itchy, shortness of breath), sadness, depression, anger	VALIDATE: Skill 1: Label emotions; use validation statement Skill 2: Willingness Hands practice with a mantra Skill 3: Self-Compassion practice
THOUGHTS: *Nobody cares! I'm all alone in the world. Not fair! People should pay attention to me if I'm suffering!*	CHECK: Skill 1: Notice: mind warps, catastrophizing, mind reading, and judging Skill 2: Ask: Is the thought 100 percent true? Skill 3: Compassionately reframe
ACTION IMPULSES: Seek reassurance (text or call until I get support), lash out, procrastinate on homework (or sleep, surf social media, smoke)	CHANGE: Skill 1: Ice, shower, or bath Skill 2: Paced Breathing practice Skill 3: Do opposite action, review factors to consider in choosing whose discomfort, VAR my needs

Patterns and Practices for Castle Dwellers: Nina

Castle girl Nina's problems stemmed from her tendency to overregulate. Her perfectionism autopilot habits kept her so far away from her emotions that she wasn't able to access them as a source of information, motivation, and connection with others. This left her with a numbed feeling of not really knowing what she cared about deeply and bursts of anxiety and frustration triggered by uncertainty. Her reactions also made it difficult for her to connect and assert herself with others, thus contributing to the lack of support she was experiencing at her job.

If you've been relating more to Nina, you might consider some of the skills we added to her practice plan for yourself. As you can see, the skills Nina chose are more about leaning into, exposing herself to, and listening to the messages of emotions. Self-compassion practices were essential for her (and you) to counter self-judgment and build the felt sense of connection to her own suffering as part of the universal human experience. The essential practice was for her to learn, from her own experience, that feelings of doubt, anxiety, or disappointment are okay. She can handle it because she's been practicing, and so can you! She also practiced Visualizing Success related to her newfound value to practice with her uncertainty passenger. Nina added establishing levels of commitment to remind her to avoid setting herself up for pass-fail scenarios, which only added to her anxiety and avoidance. At home, she also began a formal meditation practice to actively build her willingness to attend to herself in this kinder way.

Table 12.2. *Nina's Mindful-Mastery Practice Plan*

TRUE NORTH: Authenticity and supportive relationships	
FACTS: New tasks or social situations, showing vulnerability	
AUTOPILOT	**MINDFUL-MASTERY**
EMOTIONS: Doubt, anxiety, frustration	**VALIDATE:** Skill 1: Self-Compassion and Taking Roll Call practices Skill 2: Breath, Body, Sound Meditation Skill 3: Visualizing Success practice
THOUGHTS: *If I don't know, I'll fail!* Mind reading: *If I ask, I'll be smothered.* Minimization thoughts such as, *I don't care.*	**CHECK:** Skill 1: Notice when I'm distracting myself and future tripping, and redirect attention to my body Skill 2: Notice minimization and mind reading Skill 3: Check the facts
ACTION IMPULSES: Push myself harder, procrastinate, avoid new or intimate social situations	**CHANGE:** Skill 1: Self-care: Loving-Kindness Meditation Skill 2: Opposite action: don't avoid. Set levels of commitment Skill 3: VAR my needs, my values commitment

Patterns and Practices for Vulnerable Castles: Amy

Amy's passion for life often made it challenging for her to slow down and make more mindful decisions. Her pattern tended to start with pleasant feelings of excitement and enthusiasm for a project but then led to growing anxiety and frustration, ultimately burning herself (and others) out. Her patterns contributed to ups and downs in her mood, which made maintaining commitments and relationships all the more difficult. Amy needed skills to help her slow down and catch the red flags that signaled the presence of passenger reactivity and often led to impulsivity and overasserting herself.

Amy's skills objective was to notice when excitement began morphing into tension, particularly when more judgmental thoughts started showing up. To help prevent a dysregulation cycle, she built the Awareness and Acceptance Mantra into her daily practice. This helped her slow down and check the facts and factors to consider (table 11.1) before taking any action to assert herself. She also identified a hierarchy and levels of commitment to get her moving on getting another job. Because she tended to experience cyclic ups and downs in her mood, self-care skills were a must to maintain equilibrium in her sensitive vehicle. At home, she practiced Loving-Kindness Meditation to help her build a felt sense of kinder connection (rather than competition) with others. Practicing Bring It On! was a goal she set to get better at skillfully moving in and out of difficult emotions, rather than getting stuck in full throttle one way or the other.

Table 12.3. *Amy's Mindful-Mastery Practice Plan*

TRUE NORTH: Work-life balance (creativity, money security, relationship, philanthropy)

FACTS: Situations where I might worry about my position of power: authority figures, my relationship, finding a new job

AUTOPILOT	MINDFUL-MASTERY
EMOTIONS: Excitement, interest, enthusiasm, anxiety, envy, frustration, anger, exhaustion, depression	**VALIDATE:** Skill 1: Self-Compassion practice, Loving-Kindness Meditation Skill 2: Review my validation statement Skill 3: Bring It On! practice
THOUGHTS: *I can do it. If I don't hold the power, they will disrespect me.* Judging: Finding things wrong with others	**CHECK:** Skill 1: Practice the Awareness and Acceptance Mantra Skill 2: Check the facts and factors to consider in choosing whose discomfort Skill 3: Compassionately reframe
ACTION IMPULSES: Take control, assert, self-promote, nitpick, complain Overeat, isolate, ignore self-care, oversleep	**CHANGE:** Skill 1: Self-care: meditate, do yoga, cook healthy dinners, go to sleep on time. Skill 2: Opposite action Skill 3: Committed action (levels of commitment)

Building Your Own Mindful-Mastery Practice Plan

Now it's time to outline your own Mindful-Mastery Practice Plan. Using some key words, write down the values you identified in chapter 6 and the most common facts related to triggering moments at the top. Next, list the most common patterns of emotions (with any prevalent bodily sensations), thoughts, and action impulses you've identified in the left column.

Your next step is to sort through the skills you found most helpful from chapters 8 through 11 and add them to the right column. Match your validate, check, and change skills to your ETA pattern in such a way that it helps you choose the skillful alternative to each component. If you relate most to Nina and tend to try to overregulate (avoid, suppress, and change your emotions), your goal is to emphasize skills that help you lean in and validate your (and others') emotions. On the other hand, if you tend to become underregulated and intensity gets very high, like Jessica, you can start with behavior-change skills to help you self-regulate first.

PAUSE. If you could use a bit more guidance on how to go through the steps from identifying patterns to completing your Mindful-Mastery Practice Plan, this QR code will link you to a video tutorial. If you still have questions, I hope you'll sign up for the Skill Weekly newsletter at http://www.mindful-mastery.com, where you can reach out to me and I can respond to any questions and comments you might have!

Ultimately, the prescription for a healthy and flexible emotion regulation system will always include a balance of validating emotions, checking thoughts, and changing actions. Being skillful means building a better relationship with your passengers, like an excellent parent, caring for them with kindness *and* not letting them run the show! Your Mindful-Mastery Practice Plan will remind you how to more kindly attend to them while helping you maintain your commitments to what's important. Keep practicing, and you will build a life far beyond just adulting; you will be on your way to mastering adulthood!

Check Engine! Service Needed

We all have unique red-flag warning signs that signal a need to return to our skills. Reflecting on your dashboards, what are some signs and symptoms showing that you need to attend to your mind-body vehicle? The most obvious red flags can often be found in your actions, for example your self-care starts slipping, or you're getting into more arguments, showing up late to work, or just less motivated. How do you know when your emotional resilience is slipping? Take a moment to really think about your particular red flags. Write these down on the back of your practice plan or on something you will see every day.

PAUSE. Where might you keep a copy of your practice plan handy so you can refer to it frequently?

Referring Back to the Owner's Manual

Oh my gosh, we're finished! I'm imagining you out there having completed this intense and illuminating process for yourself. And I couldn't be more proud of you! As you've seen, this isn't the kind of book you can just skim through, check the box, and say, "Done!" This thing called mastering adulthood is an ongoing journey of self-discovery.

Going beyond adulting is a constant process of figuring out what works to move you forward and using your mindfulness skills to notice when something that once worked no longer does. The components on your dashboards and prescription for mindful-mastery will stay the same, but the content will be ever-changing, just like you are. So I hope you will continue to check in here and online at http://www.mindful-mastery .com for updates from time to time in the service of maintaining your mind-body vehicle.

It has been an honor to be your guide in this process. If you take one last message with you, let it be this: The road is long. Your path will change. Your own true-north values will guide you where to go next. There will be detours. That's okay. As long as you keep your eyes on your values, you'll find your way back to your path. Be kind with your emotions, hold your thoughts lightly, and stay close to your commitments.

May you BE well,

Lara

Acknowledgments

On a Wednesday night in the winter of 2017, I stood in my hallway, arms crossed, brow furrowed. With my lower lip protruded, I literally stomped my foot and whined, "My book is never going to get published!" I was just recovering from an illness, and began to lose faith that the drafts upon drafts I had begun would ever end up anywhere other than the dustbin of my hard drive.

As fate would have it, during a supervision meeting with a student the very next morning, an email arrived from the woman who is responsible for this book you are holding.

> Dear Dr. Fielding,
> I am an acquisitions editor at New Harbinger Publications.
> I came across your articles and blog and am inspired by your important work in mindfulness-based cognitive therapy, and your website, Mindful Mastery. I'm writing to inquire whether you would consider writing a book on mindfulness and emotion regulation for New Harbinger. If you're open to it, I would love to explore this idea with you.

I was so dumbfounded; I actually asked my student if the email said what I thought it did. I am, of course, eternally grateful to Elizabeth Hollis Hansen for taking a chance on this first-time author and stewarding me into the expedition that became *Mastering Adulthood*.

Throughout the process of this book, from conception to delivery, I have referred to this work as my child: conceived from my own experience and the wisdom passed down by luminaries in the field of third wave Cognitive Behavioral Therapies. In particular, thank you to the visionary minds of Steven Hayes, PhD, and Marsha Linehan, PhD, the founding developers of Acceptance and Commitment Therapy (ACT) and Dialectical Behavior Therapy (DBT) respectively, upon which this book is based.

Before embarking on this journey, I never could have imagined how much it really does take a village to get an idea from one's head to the words you are reading right now. I am so very grateful to everyone in the New Harbinger family for helping me deliver this labor of love! It was Caleb Beckwith that coached me to hone my message and get clearer in its articulation. Thank you for your patience and detailed feedback to help me clear the weeds from my head, and for going to bat for me and bringing the new and innovative QR codes into reality. Even with the weeds cleared and the message coming through, the focused eye of Gretel Hakansan was still crucial to remedy my lifelong struggle with attention to detail. Thank you so much for taking an extra run through to get me across the finish line!

And, as great as the team made the inside, the sizzling cover design and title brought the whole package to life! Thank you to Amy Shoup and the art direction team for going the extra mile to find the perfect cover design! Thank you also to everyone at New Harbinger who collaborated to come up with a title that so engagingly and succinctly highlights the aims of the book.

Also, to all the teachers I have encountered along the way, thank you. I conceived and delivered this book for those who are caught in the struggle with the traps our minds create. To those I have loved, but could not help, I am grateful for the lessons you taught me, and hopeful that this book may help others overcome the hurdles on their way to *Mastering Adulthood*.

References

Adlard, P. A., and C. W. Cotman. 2004. "Voluntary Exercise Protects Against Stress-Induced Decreases in Brain-Derived Neurotrophic Factor Protein Expression." *Neuroscience* 124: 985–992.

Allen, M. 2000. "The Psychobiology of Athletic Training." In *Sport Psychiatry: Theory and Practice*, edited by D. Begel and R. W. Burton. New York: W. W. Norton and Company.

American Psychological Association. 2017. "Stress in America: The State of Our Nation," November 1. Retrieved from http://www.apa.org/news/press/releases/stress/2017/state-nation.pdf.

American Psychological Association. 2018. "Stress in America: Uncertainty about Health Care," January 24. Retrieved from http://www.apa.org/news/press/releases/stress/2017/uncertainty-health-care.pdf.

Arch, J. J., and M. G. Craske. 2006. "Mechanisms of Mindfulness: Emotion Regulation Following a Focused Breathing Induction." *Behaviour Research and Therapy* 44(12): 1849–1858.

Arnett, J. J. 2004. *Emerging Adulthood: The Winding Road from the Late Teens Through the Twenties.* Oxford: Oxford University Press.

Baer, R. A., G. T. Smith, J. Hopkins, J. Krietemeyer, and L. Toney. 2006. "Using Self-Report Assessment Methods to Explore Facets of Mindfulness." *Assessment* 13(1): 27–45.

Barbour, K. A., T. M. Edenfield, and J. A. Blumenthal. 2007. "Exercise as a Treatment for Depression and Other Psychiatric Disorders: A Review." *Journal of Cardiopulmonary Rehabilitation and Prevention* 27(6): 359–367.

Bishop, S. R., M. Lau, S. Shapiro, L. Carlson, N. D. Anderson, J. Carmody, Z. V. Segal, S. Abbey, M. Speca, D. Velting, and G. Devins. 2004. "Mindfulness: A Proposed Operational Definition." *Clinical Psychology: Science and Practice* 11(30): 230–241.

Bland, J. 2017. "Defining Function in the Functional Medicine Model." *Integrative Medicine (Encinitas)* 16(1): 22–25.

Boardman, J. D., and K. B. Alexander. 2011. "Stress Trajectories, Health Behaviors, and the Mental Health of Black and White Young Adults." *Social Science and Medicine* 72(10): 1659–1666, http://doi.org/10.1016/j.socscimed.2011.03.024.

Campbell-Sills, L., D. H. Barlow, T. A. Brown, and S. G. Hofmann. 2006. "Effects of Suppression and Acceptance on Emotional Responses of Individuals with Anxiety and Mood Disorders." *Behaviour Research and Therapy* 44(9): 1251–1263.

Camrody, J., and R. Baer. 2008. "Relationships Between Mindfulness Practice and Levels of Mindfulness, Medical and Psychological Symptoms and Well-Being in a Mindfulness-Based Stress Reduction Program." *Journal of Behavioral Medicine* 31(1): 23–33.

Carleton, R. N. 2016. "Fear of the Unknown: One Fear to Rule Them All." *Journal of Anxiety Disorders* 31: 5–21.

Carleton, R. N. 2018, January 8. Personal Interview.

Cash, M., and K. Whittingham. 2010. "What Facets of Mindfulness Contribute to Psychological Well-Being and Depressive, Anxious, and Stress-Related Symptomatology?" *Mindfulness* 1(3): 177–182. http://doi.org/10.1007/s12 671-010-0023-4.

Cater, R. E., II. 1995. "Chronic Intestinal Candidiasis as a Possible Etiological Factor in the Chronic Fatigue Syndrome." *Medical Hypotheses* 44(6): 507–515.

Conway, K. P., W. Compton, F. S. Stinson, and B. F. Grant. 2006. "Lifetime Comorbidity of DSM-IV Mood and Anxiety Disorders and Specific Drug Use Disorders: Results from the National Epidemiologic Survey on Alcohol and Related Conditions." *Journal of Clinical Psychiatry* 67(2): 247–257.

Craske, M. G. 2013. *Optimizing Exposure Therapy for Your Anxiety Disorders.* Personal Collection of Michele G. Craske, University of California, Los Angeles.

Crosby, J. M., A. B. Armstrong, M. A. Nafziger, and M. P. Twohig. 2013. "Using Acceptance and Commitment Therapy (ACT) to Treat Perfectionism in College Students." In *Mindfulness and Acceptance for Counseling College Students,* 139–158, edited by J. Pistorello. Oakland, CA: New Harbinger Publications.

Curran, T., A. P. Hill, and L. J. Williams. 2017. "The Relationships Between Conditional Regard and Adolescents' Self-Critical and Narcissistic Perfectionism." *Personality and Individual Differences* 109: 17–22, http://dx.doi.org/10.1016/j.paid.2016.12.035.

Dalton, E. D. 2017. "Explication of the Relationship Between Depressive Symptoms, Stress, and Health Behaviors in Young Adults." PhD dissertation, University of California, Los Angeles.

De Berker, A. O., R. B. Rutledge, C. Mathys, L. Marshal, G. F. Cross, R. J. Dolan, and S. Bestmann. 2016. "Computations of Uncertainty Mediate Acute Stress Responses in Humans." *Nature Communications* 7: 10996.

DiNicolantonio, J. J., V. Mehta, N. Onkaramurthy, and H. O'Keefe, H. 2017. "Fructose-Induced Inflammation and Increased Cortisol: A New Mechanism for How Sugar Induces Visceral Adiposity." *Progress in Cardiovascular Diseases.* https://doi.org/10.1016/j.pcad.2017.12.001.

Dunn, A. L., M. H. Trivedi, J. B. Kampert, C. G. Clark, and H. O. Chambliss. 2005. "Exercise Treatment for Depression: Efficacy and Dose Response." *American Journal of Preventative Medicine* 28(1): 1–8.

Dunn, A. L., M. H. Trivedi, and H. A. O'Neal. 2001. "Physical Activity Dose-Response Effects on Outcomes of Depression and Anxiety." *Medicine and Science in Sports and Exercise* 33(6): S587–S597.

Eifert, G. H., and M. Heffner. 2003. "The Effects of Acceptance Versus Control Contexts on Avoidance of Panic-Related Symptoms." *Journal of Behavior Therapy and Experimental Psychiatry* 34(3–4): 293–312.

Erisman, S. M., and L. Roemer. 2010. "A Preliminary Investigation of the Effects of Experimentally Induced Mindfulness on Emotional Responding to Film Clips." *Emotion* 10(1): 72–82.

Ernst, C., A. K. Olson, J. P. J. Pinel, R. W. Lam, and B. R. Christie. 2006. "Antidepressant Effects of Exercise: Evidence for an Adult-Neurogenesis Hypothesis?" *Journal of Psychiatry and Neuroscience* 31(2): 84–92.

Fardouly, J., P. C. Diedrichs, L. R. Vartanian, and E. Halliwell. 2015. "Social Comparisons on Social Media: The Impact of Facebook on Young Women's Body Image Concerns and Mood." *Body Image* 13: 38–45.

Festinger, L. 1954. "A Theory of Social Comparison Processes." *Human Relations* 7(2): 117–140.

Finucane, A., and S. Mercer. 2006. "An Exploratory Mixed Methods Study of the Acceptability and Effectiveness of Mindfulness-Based Cognitive Therapy for Patients with Active Depression and Anxiety in Primary Care." *BMC Psychiatry* 6: 1–14.

Follette, V. M., and J. Pistorello. 2007. *Finding Life Beyond Trauma: Using Acceptance and Commitment Therapy to Heal from Post-Traumatic Stress and Trauma-Related Problems.* Oakland, CA: New Harbinger Publications.

Fruzzetti, A. E., C. Shenk, and P. S. Hoffman. 2005. "Family Interaction and the Development of Borderline Personality Disorder: A Transactional Model." *Development and Psychopathology* 17(4): 1007–1030, http://doi.org/10.1017/S0954579405050479.

Gable, S. I., and E. A. Impett. 2012. "Approach and Avoidance Motives and Close Relationships." *Social and Personality Psychology Compass* 6(1): 95–108.

Gillett, D. A., and S. J. Mazza. 2018. "Clarifying a Construct: An Integrative Functional Model of Reassurance-Seeking Behaviors." *Journal of Rational-Emotional and Cognitive Behavior Therapy*, https://doi.org/10.1007/s10942-018-0291-9.

Gleeson, M., N. C. Bishop, D. J. Stensel, M. R. Lindley, S. S. Mastana, and M. A. Nimmo. 2011. "The Anti-Inflammatory Effects of Exercise: Mechanisms and Implications for the Prevention and Treatment of Disease." *Nature Reviews Immunology* 11(9): 607–615, http://doi.org/10.1038/nri3041.

Goldberg, S. B., R. P. Tucker, P. A. Greene, R. J. Davidson, B. E. Wampold, D. J. Kearney, and T. L. Simpson. 2018. "Mindfulness-Based Interventions for Psychiatric Disorders: A Systematic Review and Meta-Analysis." *Clinical Psychology Review* 59: 52–60, http://dx.doi.org/10.1016/j.cpr.2017.10.011.

Greenberger, D., and C. A. Padesky. 1995. *Mind Over Mood: Change How You Feel by Changing the Way You Think.* New York, NY: Guilford Press.

Gross, J. J., and R. F. Munoz. 1995. "Emotion Regulation and Mental Health." *Clinical Psychological: Science and Practice* 2: 151–164.

Han, T. L., R. D. Cannon, and S. G. Villas-Bôas. 2011. "The Metabolic Basis of *Candida albicans* Morphogenesis and Quorum Sensing." *Fungal Genetics and Biology* 48(8): 747–763, http://doi.org/10.1016/j.fgb.2011.04.002.

Hatchard, T., O. Mioduszewski, A. Zambrana, E. O'Farrell, M. Caluyong, P. A. Poulin, and A. M. Smith. 2017. "Neural Changes Associated with Mindfulness-Based Stress Reduction (MBSR): Current Knowledge, Limitations, and Future Directions." *Psychology and Neuroscience* 10(1): 41–56.

Hayes, S. C. 2016. Psychological Flexibility: How Love Turns Pain into Purpose. TED Talk. Retrieved from https://www.youtube.com/watch?v=o79_gmO5ppg.

Hayes, S. C., J. B. Luoma, F. W. Bond, A. Masuda, and J. Lillis. 2006. "Acceptance and Commitment Therapy: Model, Processes and Outcomes." *Behaviour Research and Therapy* 44(1): 1–25.

Hayes, S. C., and S. Smith. 2005. *Get Out of Your Mind and into Your Life: The New Acceptance and Commitment Therapy.* Oakland, CA: New Harbinger Publications.

Hayes, S. C., K. D. Strosahl, and K. G. Wilson. 1999. *Acceptance and Commitment Therapy: An Experiential Approach to Behavior Change.* New York: Guilford Press.

Hayes, S. C., K. D. Strosahl, and K. G. Wilson. 2003. *Acceptance and Commitment Therapy: An Experiential Approach to Behavior Change.* New York. Guilford Press.

Hyman, M. 2009. *The Ultra Mind Solution: Fix Your Broken Brain by Healing Your Body First.* New York: Scribner.

Kabat-Zinn, J. 1990. *Full Catastrophe Living: Using the Wisdom of your Body and Mind to Face Stress, Pain, and Illness.* New York: Delacourt Press.

Kabat-Zinn, J. 1996. "Mindfulness Meditation: What It Is, What It Isn't, and Its Role in Health Care and Medicine." In *Comparative and Psychological Study on Meditation,* edited by Y. Haruki, Y. Ishii, and M. Suzuki. Eburon, Netherlands: MBSR Training Materials.

Khurana R. K., S. Watabiki, J. Hebel, R. Toro, and E. Nelson. 1980. "Cold Face Test in the Assessment of Trigeminal-Brainstem-Vagal Function in Humans." *Annals of Neurology* 7(2): 144–149.

Kiecolt-Glaser, J. K., and S. J. Wilson. 2017. "Lovesick: How Couples' Relationships Influence Health." *Annual Review of Clinical Psychology* 13(1): 421–433.

Kohut, M. L., D. A. McCann, D. W. Russell, D. N. Konopka, J. E. Cunnick, W. D. Franke, M. C. Castillo, A. E. Reighard, and E. Vanderah. 2005. "Aerobic Exercise, but Not Flexibility/Resistance Exercise, Reduces Serum IL-18, CRP, and IL-6 Independent of Beta Blockers, BMI, and Psychosocial Factors in Older Adults." *Brain, Behavior, and Immunity* 20(3): 201–209.

Kotsou, I., C. Leys, and P. Fossion. 2018. "Acceptance Alone Is a Better Predictor of Psychopathology and Well-Being Than Emotional Competence, Emotion Regulation and Mindfulness." *Journal of Affective Disorders* 226: 142–145.

Kraft, T. L., and S. D. Pressman. 2012. "Grin and Bear It: The Influence of Manipulated Facial Expression on the Stress Response." *Psychological Science* 23(11): 1372–1378.

LeMoyne, T., and T. Buchanan. 2011. "Does 'Hovering' Matter? Helicopter Parenting and Its Effect on Well-Being." *Sociological Spectrum* 31: 399–418.

Lin, L., J. E. Sidani, A. Shensa, A. Radovic, E. Miller, J. B. Colditz, B. L. Hoffman, L. M. Giles, and B. A. Primack. 2016. "Association Between Social Media Use and Depression Among U.S. Young Adults." *Depression and Anxiety* 33(4): 323–331.

Linehan, M. 1993a. *Cognitive-Behavioral Treatment of Borderline Personality Disorder.* New York: Guilford Press.

Linehan, M. 1993b. *Skills Training Manual for Treating Borderline Personality Disorder.* New York: Guilford Press.

LinkedIn. 2017. "New LinkedIn Research Shows 75 Percent of 25–33 Year Olds Have Experienced Quarter-Life Crises," November 17. Retrieved from https://news.linkedin.com/2017/11/new-linkedin-research-shows-75-percent-of-25-33-year-olds-have-e.

Lipman, F. 2018. *How to Be Well: The 6 Keys to a Happy and Healthy Life.* New York: Houghton Mifflin.

Liu, R. T. 2017. "The Microbiome as a Novel Paradigm in Studying Stress and Mental Health." *American Psychologist* 72(7): 665–667.

Luyten, P., and S. J. Blatt. 2013. "Interpersonal Relatedness and Self-Definition in Normal and Disrupted Personality Development." *American Psychologist* 68(3): 172–183.

Lynch, T. R. 2018. *Radically Open Dialectical Behavior Therapy: Theory and Practice for Treating Disorders of Overcontrol.* Oakland, CA: Context Press.

Markus, H. 1978. "The Effect of Mere Presence on Social Facilitation: An Unobtrusive Test." *Journal of Experimental Social Psychology* 14(4): 389–397.

Markus, R., G. Panhuysen, A. Tuiten, and H. Koppeschaar. 2000. "Effects of Food on Cortisol and Mood in Vulnerable Subjects Under Controllable and Uncontrollable Stress." *Physiology and Behavior* 70(3–4): 333–342.

Masuda, A., S. C. Hayes, M. P Twohig, C. Drossel, J. Lillis, and Y. Washio. 2009. "A Parametric Study of Cognitive Defusion and the Believability and Discomfort of Negative Self-Relevant Thoughts." *Behavior Modification* 33(2): 250–262.

Mayer, E. 2016. *The Mind-Gut Connection: How the Hidden Conversation Within Our Bodies Impacts Our Mood, Our Choices, and Our Overall Health.* New York: HarperCollins.

Mayer, E. A., R. Knight, S. K. Mazmanian, J. F. Cryan, and K. Tillisch. 2014. "Gut Microbes and the Brain: Paradigm Shift in Neuroscience." *The Journal of Neuroscience* 34(46): 15490–15496, http://dx.doi.org/10.1523/JNEUROSCI.3299-14.2014.

McNamara, R. K., and S. W. Carlson. 2006. "Role of Omega-3 Fatty Acids in Brain Development and Function: Potential Implications for the Pathogenesis and Prevention of Psychopathology." *Prostaglandins, Leukotrienes and Essential Fatty Acids* 75(4–5): 329–349.

Menezes, C. B., and L. Bizarro. 2015. "Effects of Focused Meditation on Difficulties in Emotion Regulation and Trait Anxiety." *Psychology and Neuroscience* 8(3): 350–365, http://dx.doi.org/10.1037/pne0000015.

Moscovitch, D. A. 2009. "What Is the Core Fear in Social Phobia?: A New Model to Facilitate Individualized Case Conceptualization and Treatment." *Cognitive and Behavioral Practice* 16: 123–134.

Mroczek, D. K., and D. M. Almeida. 2004. "The Effect of Daily Stress, Personality, and Age on Daily Negative Affect." *Journal of Personality* 72(2): 355–378, http://doi.org/10.1111/j.0022-3506.2004.00265.x.

Najmi, S., and D. M. Wegner. 2008. "Thought Suppression and Psychopathology." In *Handbook of Approach and Avoidance Motivation*, edited by A. J. Elliott. New York: Psychology Press.

Neff, K., and C. Germer. 2017. "Self-Compassion and Psychological Wellbeing." In *The Oxford Handbook of Compassion Science* 371–386. edited by E. M. Seppälä, E. Simon-Thomas, S. L. Brown, et al. Oxford: Oxford University Press.

Nelson, L. J., L. M. Padilla-Walker, and M. G. Nielson. 2015. "Is Hovering Smothering or Loving? An Examination of Parental Warmth as a Moderator of Relations Between Helicopter Parenting and Emerging Adults' Indices of Adjustment." *Emerging Adulthood* 3(4): 282–285.

Ng, Q. X., C. Peters, C. Y. X. Ho, D. Y., Lim, and W. S. Yeo. 2018. "A Meta-Analysis of the Use of Probiotics to Alleviate Depressive Symptoms." *Journal of Affective Disorders* 228: 13–19.

Niles, A. N., M. G. Craske, M. D. Lieberman, and C. Hur. 2015. "Affect Labeling Enhances Exposure Effectiveness for Public Speaking Anxiety." *Behaviour Research and Therapy* 68: 27–36.

Orme-Johnson, D. W., and V. A. Barnes. 2014. "Effects of the Transcendental Meditation Technique on Trait Anxiety: A Meta-Analysis of Randomized Controlled Trials." *The Journal of Alternative and Complementary Medicine* 20(5): 330–341.

Osborn, A. 2017. *Allison Osborn: Why Are Millennials So Stressed? Is It Quarter Life Crisis?* TED Talk Video, Retrieved from https://www.youtube.com/watch?v=cwASai4hTZU.

Palmer, C. A., and C. A. Alfano. 2017. "Sleep and Emotion Regulation: An Organizing, Integrative Review." *Sleep Medicine Reviews* 31: 6–16.

Parker, K., and G. Livingston. 2014. "6 Facts About American Fathers." Pew Research Center.

Pascoe, M. C., and Bauer, I. E. 2015. "A Systemic Review of Randomized Control Trials on the Effects of Yoga on Stress Measures and Mood." *Journal of Psychiatric Research* 68: 270–282. http://dx.doi.org/10.1016/j .jpsychires.2015.07.013.

Plonsker, R., D. Gavish Biran, A. Zvielli, and A. Bernstein. 2017. "Cognitive Fusion and Emotion Differentiation: Does Getting Entangled with Our Thoughts Dysregulate the Generation, Experience and Regulation of Emotion?" *Cognition and Emotion* 31(6): 1286–1293.

Primack B. A., A. Shensa, J. E. Sidani, E. O. Whaite, L. Y. Lin, D. Rosen, J. B. Colditz, A. Radovic, and E. Miller. 2017. "Social Media Use and Perceived Social Isolation Among Young Adults in the U.S." *American Journal of Preventative Medicine* 53(1): 1–8.

Quello, S. B., K. T. Brady, and S. C. Sonne. 2005. "Mood Disorders and Substance Abuse Disorder: A Complex Comorbidity." *Science and Practice Perspectives* 3(1): 13–24.

Rahl, H. A., E. K. Lindsay, L. E. Pacilio, K. W. Brown, and D. J. Creswell. 2017. "Brief Mindfulness Meditation Training Reduces Mind Wandering: The Critical Role of Acceptance." *Emotion* 17(2): 224–230.

Russo-Neustadt, A., T. Ha, R. Ramirez, and J. P. Kesslak. 2001. "Physical Activity–Antidepressant Treatment Combination: Impact on Brain-Derived Neurotrophic Factor and Behavior in an Animal Model." *Behavioural Brain Research* 120(1): 87–95.

Sapolsky, R. M. 2003. "Stress and Plasticity in the Limbic System." *Neurochemical Research* 28(11): 1735–1742.

Schiffrin, H. H., M. Liss, H. Miles-McLean, K. A. Geary, M. J. Erchull, and T. Tashner. 2014. "Helping or Hovering? The Effects of Helicopter Parenting on College Students' Well-Being." *Journal of Child and Family Studies* 23(3): 548–557.

Soh, N., Walter, G., Baur, L., and Collins, C. 2009. "Nutrition, Mood, and Behaviour: A Review." *Acta Neuropsychiatrica* 21(5): 214–227. doi: 10.1111 /j.1601–5215.2009.00413.x.

Stonerock, G. L., B. M. Hoffman, P. J. Smith, and J. A. Blumenthal. 2015. *"Exercise as Treatment for Anxiety: Systematic Review and Analysis." Annals of Behavioral Medicine* 49(4): 542–556.

Sturrock, B., and D. Mellor. 2013. "Perceived Emotional Invalidation and Borderline Personality Disorder Features: A Test of Theory." *Personality and Mental Health* 8(2): 128–142, http://doi.org/10.1002/pmh.1249.

Swing, E. L., D. A. Gentile, C. A. Anderson, and D. A. Walsh. 2010. "Television and Video Game Exposure and the Development of Attention Problems." *Pediatrics* 126(2): 214–221.

Torre, J. B., and M. D. Lieberman. 2018. "Putting Feelings into Words: Affect Labeling as Implicit Emotion Regulation." *Emotion Review* 10(2): 1–9, http://doi.org/10.1177/1754073917742706.

Traustadóttir, T., P. R. Bosch, and K. S. Matt. 2005. "The HPA Axis Response to Stress in Women: Effects of Aging and Fitness." *Psychoneuroendocrinology* 30(4): 392–402.

Ulz, S., N. Muscanell, and C. Khalid. 2015. "Snapchat Elicits More Jealousy Than Facebook: A Comparison of Snapchat and Facebook Use." *Cyberpsychology, Behavior, and Social Networking* 18(3), https://doi.org/10.1089/cyber.2014.0479.

U.S. Department of Health and Human Services. 2015. "Dietary Guidelines 2015–2020 for Americans, Appendix 9: Alcohol" 8th edition, December. Washington, D.C., Retrieved from https://health.gov/dietaryguidelines/2015/guidelines/appendix-9.

Veissière, S. P. L., and M. Stendel. 2018. "Hypernatural Monitoring: A Social Rehearsal Account of Smartphone Addiction." *Frontiers in Psychology*, http://doi.org/10.3389/fpsyg.2018.00141.

Vespa, J. 2017. "The Changing Economics and Demographics of Young Adulthood: 1975–2016." Report Number: P20–579. U.S. Census Report. Retrieved from https://www.census.gov/library/publications/2017/demo/p20-579.html.

Viru, A., and M. Viru. 2004. "Cortisol—Essential Adaptation Hormone." *International Journal of Sports Medicine* 25(6): 461–464.

Walser, R. D., and D. Westrup. 2007. *Acceptance and Commitment Therapy for the Treatment of Post-Traumatic Stress Disorder and Trauma-Related Problems: A Practitioner's Guide to Using Mindfulness and Acceptance Strategies.* Oakland, CA. New Harbinger Publications.

Winnebeck, E., M. Fissler, M. Gärtner, P. Chadwick, and T, Barnhofer. 2017. "Training in Mindfulness Meditation Reduces Symptoms in Patients with Chronic or Recurrent Lifetime History of Depression: A Randomized Controlled Study." *Behaviour Research and Therapy* 99: 124–130.

Zeng, X., C. P. K. Chiu, R. Wang, T. P. S. Oei, and F. Y. K. Leung. 2015. "The Effect of Loving-Kindness Meditation on Positive Emotions: A Meta-analytic Review." *Frontiers in Psychology* 6: 1623.

Lara E. Fielding, PsyD, is a psychologist who specializes in using mindfulness-based therapies to manage stress and strong emotions. She studied the psychophysiology of stress and emotions at the University of California, Los Angeles; and Harvard; before getting her doctorate at Pepperdine University graduate school of education and psychology, where she is currently adjunct professor.

In her private practice in Beverly Hills, CA, she specializes in treating young adults challenged by the stresses of transitioning roles and responsibilities resulting in difficulties with mood, motivation, and emotion regulation. Her values mission, and aim of her work, is to empower young adults through self-awareness, bridge the gap between research and people, and lower barriers to the availability of science-based mental health interventions. She frequently offers trainings in the community, and freely shares the skills she teaches in her blogs on *Thrive Global, Psych Central,* and Youtube.

Register your **new harbinger** titles for additional benefits!

When you register your **new harbinger** title—purchased in any format, from any source—you get access to benefits like the following:

- Downloadable accessories like printable worksheets and extra content

- Instructional videos and audio files

- Information about updates, corrections, and new editions

Not every title has accessories, but we're adding new material all the time.

Access free accessories in 3 easy steps:

1. Sign in at NewHarbinger.com (or **register** to create an account).

2. Click on **register a book**. Search for your title and click the **register** button when it appears.

3. Click on the **book cover or title** to go to its details page. Click on **accessories** to view and access files.

That's all there is to it!

If you need help, visit:

NewHarbinger.com/accessories

new harbinger
CELEBRATING
40 YEARS